ENTRANCE TO THE GOLDEN GATE.

CALIFORNIA LIFE

ILLUSTRATED.

By WILLIAM TAYLOR,
OF THE CALIFORNIA CONFERENCE,
AUTHOR OF "SEVEN YEARS' STREET PREACHING IN SAN FRANCISCO" AND "ADDRESS TO YOUNG AMERICA."

When a traveler returneth home, let him not leave the countries where he hath traveled altogether behind him.—Lord Bacon.

Then shalt thou lay up gold as dust, and the gold of Ophir as the stones of the brooks.—Job xxii, 24.

SIXTEEN ENGRAVINGS.

New-York:
PUBLISHED FOR THE AUTHOR,
BY CARLTON & PORTER, 200 MULBERRY-STREET.
1858.

CONTENTS.

CHAPTER I.

MISSIONARY LIFE.

CHAPTER II.

MISSIONARY LIFE — CONTINUED.

CHAPTER III.

MISSIONARY LIFE — CONTINUED.

CHAPTER IV.

MISSIONARY LIFE — CONTINUED.

CHAPTER V.

MISSIONARY LIFE — CONTINUED.

CHAPTER VI.

SOCIAL LIFE IN CALIFORNIA.

CHAPTER VII.

SOCIAL LIFE—CONTINUED.

CHAPTER VIII.

HOSPITAL REMINISCENCES.

CHAPTER IX.

EXTENT AND RESOURCES OF CALIFORNIA.

CHAPTER X.

LIFE AMONG THE MINERS.

CHAPTER XI.

CALIFORNIA AS A MISSIONARY FIELD.

CHAPTER XII.

BIT OF EXPERIENCE — CONCLUSION.

LIST OF ILLUSTRATIONS.

CALIFORNIA LIFE ILLUSTRATED.

CHAPTER I.

MISSIONARY LIFE.

On the 21st day of September, 1849, the captain of our noble ship said: "We are now in latitude about five miles north of the Golden Gate. Never having entered the port of San Francisco, I thought it best to run a few miles north, and feel my way down the coast till I could find the entrance." We could at that moment distinctly hear the breakers, but were enveloped in so dense a fog that the man at the look-out could not see the length of the ship ahead. The breeze was dying away, and to proceed on our course was very hazardous, for if we should get too far "in shore," and have no wind to enable us to "tack, and wear off," a current setting in might carry us on to the rocks. We therefore "stood off" a while, hoping the fog would rise, but it did not. The breeze, however, sprang up a little, and Captain Wilson said: "We'll head on toward those breakers, and see what we can find." That shrill command, "'Bout ship," sent a thrill of commingled hope and fear to the hearts of the entire ship's company. There we were, in untried seas, running through a fog, which utterly darkened the field of vision in every direction, right toward the breakers, whose thunder pealed its warning notes into our ears with increasing distinctness as we advanced. But we had unshaken confidence in the skill of our commander, and said, "Go on." We had tried him during a long voyage round Cape Horn; had witnessed his perfect self-possession as he stood amid the wreck of our masts and rigging, which had been thrown down in tangled prostration on the deck of our noble ship by the sudden burst of a "white squall;" had seen him convert his deck into a shipyard, and make masts, yards, and rigging, and refit, without putting into port, or losing a day's sail; and again we said to our grand old captain in the fog, "Go on." So on and on we went till, as suddenly as striking a sunken reef, we ran out of the darkness into the brightest day of California's sunshine. The whole coast, as far as the eye could reach, was, in a moment, spread out to the rapturous gaze of one hundred passengers, who had not seen the land but once for one hundred and fifty-five days. The scene was transporting beyond description.

There lay the land we had longed for; over us were the brightest skies we ever had seen; around us were myriads of ducks and pelicans, and other fowls of the sea in vast variety. Beneath us were several whales spouting and playing about our ship, often coming within thirty feet of us. Some of the passengers discharged their revolvers at them without any apparent effect.

Thus entertained we sailed down the coast, ran without a pilot through the Golden Gate,* and just as the sun was sinking below the horizon of the great Pacific our sails were furled, and the command was given, "Let go the anchor."

During our voyage of five months and three days we heard no tidings from California, except at Valparaiso. There we were informed by "The latest news from San Francisco," that lawless anarchy reigned, that there was no security for life or property, and that the few families who had the bad fortune to go to California had been obliged to leave, not excepting even the family of the territorial governor. Such news reminded me of the sayings of some of my friends, who had charged me with cruelty for taking my family to that "barbarous land."

Under these circumstances we were all very anx-

* See Frontispiece.

ious to know the facts about California life. The first thing that arrested our attention after finding our moorings, by way of variety, after the frequent shouts of "Sail ho!" or, "A whale! a whale!" was the lassooing of a bullock on the north side of "Telegraph Hill," then a wild wood, now a populous part of the city of San Francisco. It was now too late for the passengers to go ashore that night, all being strangers in a strange land; but soon a Mr. M., a brother of one of our passengers, boarded our ship, and we all gathered around him to hear the news. He brought marvelous things to our ears. No war in the country, but peace and plenty, and fortunes for all who could work or gamble expertly: that clerks were getting in San Francisco two hundred dollars per month, cooks three hundred per month; the gamblers were the aristocracy of the land; gambling being the most profitable, hence the most respectable business a man could follow. I asked the gentleman whether or not there were any ministers of the Gospel or churches in the place?

"Yes," said he, "we have one preacher, but preaching won't pay here, so he quit preaching and went to gambling. There is but one church in town, and that has been converted into a jail."

Some one told him that I was a minister, and had the frame of a church aboard. He advised by all means to sell the church, assuring me that I could

SAN FRANCISCO IN 1849, FROM THE HEAD OF CLAY-STREET.

make nothing out of it as a church, but I could sell it for ten thousand dollars. I told him my church was not for sale. I afterward found his assertions in regard to wages true; in regard to the gamblers nearly true; but his ecclesiastical history false, except that the "school-house on the Plaza," which had been used as a preaching place, was then used for a jail. With our evening repast of news from Mr. M. we retired to rest, hoping on the morrow to spy out the land ourselves. The next morning, Saturday, September 22, I went ashore in company with Captain Wilson and Robert Kellan.

When we reached the summit of the hill above Clark's Point, we stopped and took a view of the city of tents. Not a brick house in the place, and but few wooden ones, and not a wharf or pier in the harbor. But for a few old adobe houses, it would have been easy to imagine that the whole city was pitched the evening before for the accommodation of a vast caravan for the night; for the city now contained a population of about twenty thousand, and I felt oppressed with the fear that under the influence of the gold attraction of the mountains, those tents might all be struck some morning, and the city suddenly leave its moorings for parts unknown. But my business ashore was to see whether I could find any lovers of Jesus, and, especially, any bearing the name of Methodist, who could tell me how the land lay, and of the whereabouts of my fellow-missionary, Rev. Isaac Owen, who had started with his family "over the plains" before I sailed from Baltimore, and whom I expected to find on my arrival. I was introduced to the business firms of Dewitt & Harrison, Bingham, Reynolds, & Co., and Finley & Co., and spoke to many other persons; and everywhere I went made diligent inquiry whether or not there were any Methodists in the city? but everywhere learned that no such creatures lived in the place, or if they did, they had neither seen nor heard of them. After prosecuting my fruitless Methodist hunt till noonday, I fell in with Captain Stetson, master of the bark Hebe, from Baltimore, and accepted his invitation to dine with him aboard his vessel. I had seen his passengers as they embarked in Baltimore for the "land of gold," and saw him set sail on his California voyage, and listened now with mournful interest to the captain's narrative of his eventful and in some respects disastrous voyage. In attempting to pass through the Straits of Magellan he had been obliged to cast anchor, and await a favorable wind to enable him to go through the Straits. While there, some of his passengers concluded to go ashore. I believe there were seven of them who had taken their guns to have a little pleasure on the frozen shores of Patagonia. But during their absence a furious gale arose, which swept the bark from her moorings. She dragged her anchors until her chains parted, and was then driven before the blast into the Atlantic Ocean.

All the captain's earnest efforts to get back to his lost men proved ineffectual. Having no anchors left, he could not make a near approach to the land, in that stormy region, so he was under the painful necessity of leaving his adventurous sportsmen to the rigors of a Cape Horn winter, and to the tender mercies of the Patagonian Indians, considered the most merciless of their kind. Happily, however, for the poor fellows, after enduring great sufferings from cold, hunger, and Indian barbarity, they finally escaped in a vessel that was passing through the Straits.

At Valparaiso the captain supplied his bark with anchors. While there he became acquainted with Rev. Dr. Vermehr, *en route* to California as a missionary from the Protestant Episcopal Church. The doctor and his family had been so badly treated on the ship in which they had rounded the Cape, that the good people of Valparaiso made up a purse for the doctor, and secured a passage for himself and family to San Francisco in the bark Hebe. Captain Stetson, as a Christian gentleman, brought them on, in comfort, to their destination.

After dinner I again went ashore, and renewed my Methodist search. Hearing some one speak of Merrill's Hotel, I was reminded of a published letter

2

I had read, from the pen of Rev. William Roberts, giving an account of his short sojourn in San Francisco, on his way, as missionary, to Oregon, in 1847; and of his having organized a little Sunday school here, appointing J. H. Merrill superintendent. It occurred to me that this might be the same Merrill; so I hastened to find Merrill's Hotel, on Stockton-street, where the City Hospital now stands.

Finding Mr. Merrill, I ascertained sure enough that he was the man referred to by Brother Roberts. He said he was not a Methodist himself, but he knew of a number of them in the city; "and yonder," said he, "is their new church," pointing to an uncovered frame on a neighboring hill.

"There is a Methodist family," continued he, "living down there in that adobe house; and Mr. Finley, the head of the family, is sick, and I have no doubt would be glad to see you."

"I will be pleased to call on them," said I.

So Mr. Merrill went with me, and introduced me to Brother and Sister Finley. I was delighted that I had found at least one good Methodist family in California, and talked very freely with Brother and Sister Finley about the interests of our common Methodism on the Pacific coast, and asked them many questions. I then had a good season of prayer at the bedside of Brother Finley; after which they frankly informed me that I was mistaken in regard to their Church relationship; that they were not Methodists exactly, but Campbellites.

I covered my disappointment as well as I could, but felt glad that I had made their acquaintance, for I had come to the conclusion that they were a kind and good family, whatever they might be called; an opinion I have never changed during a subsequent acquaintance of seven years.

As I was taking my leave of these my *first Methodist* acquaintances, I was met at the door by a plain-looking man, five feet eight, and was introduced to him as Brother John Troubody. "He is a Methodist," said Sister Finley with a smile; and such I found him to be, a *truebody* in every respect, true as a personal friend, and true to the interests of the Church. He introduced me to Rev. O. C. Wheeler, the Baptist minister of the city, who invited me to fill his pulpit the next day at 11 A. M. Brother Troubody then introduced me to Brother Asa White's family. Brother White was a local preacher from Illinois, more recently from Oregon. His sons and daughters, of whom he had a large family, were sociable and kind, and were all, except two small boys, members of the Church. They lived in the woods, in Washington-street, near Powell, in the neighborhood of where our chapel was being built. Their habitation was a small rough board house, one story high, covered with blue cotton cloth. It was known in familiar Methodist parlance, as "the shanty with the blue cover," and was the rallying point of Methodism in the city, where the prayer and class-meetings were held every Sabbath, conducted by Brother White, who had authority from Rev. William Roberts, the superintendent of the "Oregon and California Mission Conference," to do the best he could in collecting and holding the little society together till the missionary should arrive.

Brother Roberts organized a small class in San Francisco in 1847, on his way to Oregon. The class consisted of Alexander Hatler and wife, Aquila Glover and wife, and three or four others. Brother Glover was appointed the leader, but being a timid man, he never led the class after Brother Roberts left, and no class-meetings were held there, as Brother Hatler and others informed me, till the spring of 1849, when Brother White arrived from Oregon. He settled his family first in a blue tent, in the woods, near the corner of Jackson and Mason streets. Into this tent the scattered sheep were immediately gathered, and regular class-meetings were held from that time. Elihu Anthony, a local preacher, who lived a short time in the city, and then settled in Santa Cruz, assisted in these meetings, but Brother White was the responsible leader. The class numbered, upon my arrival, about twenty persons, and the traveling Methodist adventurers made an additional average attendance of about thirty.

At Brother White's I received a letter from Brother Roberts, informing me that I was appointed to San Francisco, and that my fellow-missionary, Brother Owen, was "appointed to Sacramento City and Stockton." Altogether that was to me an afternoon of thrilling interest, and contrasted hopefully with the unfruitful efforts of my forenoon adventure.

I returned to our ship in the evening with a full budget of news for the entertainment of my waiting family. Oceana, our beautiful little missionary girl, born on the South Atlantic, off "Rio de la Plata," in the region of pamperos and storms, was now about three months old. Native country she had none; the sea had been her home, the land she had never yet seen. Her mother, nearly exhausted by the monotonous wear and tear of sea life, and the wasting effects of chronic diarrhea, was hardly able to walk ashore, but the idea of getting off ship, and of finding a resting-place on the land, was so exhilarating, that the next morning, Sunday, September 23d, she accompanied me to Mr. Wheeler's church, on Washington-street, where I preached on the divinity of Jesus, from the text, "What think ye of Christ?"

There was profound attention and good order during the sermon, with one exception. A rough-looking man, a little beyond the meridian of life, seemed to take offense at my arguments in favor of the divinity of Christ, and cried out in the midst of my discourse:

"I don't believe it! I don't believe it!"

"Wait, my old friend," said I, "till I get through, and let us take it one at a time."

But he continued to mutter to those about him, till Mr. Wheeler arose and commanded him to hush instantly or leave the house! He got up abruptly, and walked out, and I proceeded.

That occasion was to me, and I believe to many, a "season of refreshing from the presence of the Lord." We dined with Brother Troubody, who then lived in a small house on Washington-street. He soon afterward built the first brick dwelling in the city, on the corner of Washington and Powell streets; a four-story house, about twenty-six by fifty feet, in which he still lives.

At three P. M. we attended class-meeting in the "shanty with the blue cover." The place was full of men, and many stood outside the door. Their experiences were characterized by originality, freshness, and thrilling interest. Some had "crossed the plains;" others were just from a voyage round Cape Horn; some had, on their passage across the Isthmus, seen scores of their friends swept away by the malignant fevers of Panama. All had seen sights, encountered dangers, made hairbreadth escapes from death, and they were overflowing with gratitude that "out of all the Lord had brought them by his love."

All had loved ones far away, who had been praying for them. Their prayers had been answered; but their friends did not dream that they, in California, were in a Methodist class-meeting. They thought that California was but another name for Pandemonium; that nothing could be done there without the consent of the god of the country, alias, the devil; and that he never would allow a Methodist class-meeting to be held there. Indeed they could hardly believe the testimony of their own senses, and realize that in California they were then enjoying an old-fashioned class-meeting. I will note an experience or two as a specimen.

Palmer, from New-York, said: "I used to be happy in God, but I backslid. When I departed from the Lord I got into trouble, and the further I went from him the more my troubles increased. Everything seemed to go ill with me, so I made up my mind to leave New-York and make a voyage round Cape Horn to California, and thus get rid of my troubles. But I had been out to sea but a few days when I found, to my sorrow, that I had brought all my troubles with me, and left all my comforts behind. My health was bad, my head and heart were sick, and my distress became intolerable. I then remembered that Jesus had said: 'Come unto me, all ye that labor and are heavy laden, and I will give you rest;' so I carried my burden to Jesus, and he took away my load of guilt and sorrow. Glory be to his name, forever! We had a long, tedious voyage, but my soul has been happy in God. As soon as I came ashore I inquired where I could find a Methodist class-meeting. I happily fell in with a man who pointed out this cabin, and said: 'That is the place you are hunting for.' Brethren, I was so glad to hear of such a place in California that I could hardly wait to walk up the hill to get here. I ran, and O how sweet it is, after being cooped up with the wicked during a long voyage round Cape Horn, to get to such a place as this! It is heaven to my soul! Glory be to God!"

The old man, with repeated exclamations of "Glory to God!" took his seat and wept aloud. They were tears of joy and gladness.

After leading the class inside the "shanty," I led the outsiders, among whom I found James Whiting, a native of Buenos Ayres, South America, who had been converted to God through the instrumentality of our missionary there, Rev. D. D. Lore. James told us a simple, sensible, touching story of his life as a shepherd boy in orphanage. He was brought up with the sheep, lived among them, slept among them in the open field; and while "watching his flocks by night" had often gazed at the stars, and thought of God, but saw no star to point him to Bethlehem. His soul was in darkness until the missionary found him and led him to Jesus. He had descended from American parents, but had never before trod North American soil, nor mingled with his Father's brethren in a class-meeting; and though there was no room for him in the house, he was contented to stand outside and listen, for he "would rather be a door-keeper in the house of God, than to dwell in the tents of wickedness." Being perfectly familiar with the Spanish language, he became a valuable helper in my work; sometimes going with me through the hospitals to talk to sick Spaniards about Jesus, and occasionally exhorting the Spanish portion of my street audiences, and giving them Bibles and tracts in their own language. He is still a member of the Methodist Episcopal Church in San Francisco, and doing well.

That was a class-meeting never to be forgotten. The rustic appearance of the men, and the pointed, lively impression of their narratives on my mind, are in my memory like a favorite old picture, to which the successive roll of years adds but increasing interest.

We spent the following week in learning California prices and modes of life, and in trying to secure a house in which to live. Captain Wilson kindly invited us to remain aboard ship until we could make arrangements for housekeeping, and allowed us the free use of his boat in passing to and from the land. The lowest price of boat hire for the shortest distance was one dollar per passenger. We learned prices in part by little experiments in buying. Mrs. Taylor said to a dealer in potatoes: "How much do you ask per peck for your potatoes?"

"We sell nothing by measure here," replied he, "for man or beast. Everything is bought and sold by weight, ma'am."

"Well, what do you ask per pound for potatoes?"

"Fifty cents per pound, ma'am."

"I'll take a pound to begin with," said she, laying down the money; and he gave her for fifty cents but one potato.

I priced some South American apples, nearly as tough as leather; fifty cents apiece. We ascertained that fresh beef was selling for fifty cents per pound; dried apples, seventy-five cents per pound; Oregon butter, two dollars fifty cents per pound; flour, fifty dollars per barrel; and provisions of every kind proportionably high. None of these things moved us, however, for we had brought with us a year's supply of all the substantials of life. The only difficulty with us was to get a house in which to live. Rev. O. C. Wheeler, I learned, was paying five hundred dollars a month rent for such a house as we needed, a small one-and-a-half story house, containing four or five rooms. That was frightful, for I only had money enough, including the missionary appropriation for our support for a year—seven hundred and fifty dollars—to pay rent, at that rate, for about two months.

There stood in the neighborhood of our chapel a one-story rough board shanty, about twelve feet square, with a shed roof of the same material, promising, altogether, but very little protection from the storms of approaching winter; but I thought as a last resort I would try and get my wife and babes into it till something better could be obtained. I learned that the rent for the shanty was forty dollars per month. I immediately applied for it, but lo! it had been secured for the personal occupancy of a reverend Episcopal brother, in "the regular succession;" and I, a poor irregular, was left to do the best I could.

I then spoke of building a little house, but lumber was selling for from three hundred to four hundred dollars per thousand feet. To pay such prices, and build a house with my little stock of funds was out of the question.

In the mean time I had my household goods and provisions taken ashore, paid ten dollars per dray-load to have them hauled up on the hill near the chapel, and there they lay piled up in the open air for a fortnight. That was prior to the advent of petty rogues in California.

On my second Sabbath, at eleven A. M., I again occupied the pulpit of Brother Wheeler, and had a gracious meeting. At three P. M. we had another great class-meeting in the "shanty with the blue cover." Many of the brethren with whom we had prayed, and sung, and shouted the Sabbath before had gone to parts unknown; but a new recruit had come in of the same sort. After class the question was raised, "How shall our preacher get a house to live in?" It was decided that the only way was to build one; and then an effort was made in the class to see how much could be raised toward that desirable end. But the sojourners "were *strapped*," and the resident brethren had subscribed all they felt able to give toward the chapel, and could do but little for a parsonage, so the effort resulted in a subscription amounting to twenty-seven dollars, perhaps enough to buy the nails and hinges. The prospect for a residence in the land of our adoption, as we supposed for life, was very dark; but I never had doubted that God sent me to California, and felt a comfortable assurance that in some way he would provide for us.

Captain Otis Webb, son of old Father Daniel Webb of the Providence Conference, though nothing himself but a high-minded outsider, (the Lord bless the outsiders! I have found among them some of the best friends I ever had in my life,) hearing of our situation, sent us word that he was building a house near our chapel, which would be finished in a week, and that we were welcome to the use of it, rent free, for a month. So after remaining a fortnight in port aboard ship, enjoying the hospitality of Captain Wilson, we moved into the new house of Captain Webb, a one-and-a-half story house, containing five rooms, and would have rented for about four hundred dollars a month. Thus the evil day, in regard to shelter, was postponed for a month at least. We were, however, without fireplace or stove; but, through a propitious dream of John B. Seidenstricker, of Baltimore city, we had a supply of table furniture, and some good ovens and skillets. About the time of our appointment as missionaries to California, John dreamed one night that he had given us free access to his hardware store for a supply of everything we might need in our new home; so in the morning when he awoke he dressed himself, and hastened immediately to tell us his dream and give it a practical fulfillment, which he did with a free good-will. The Lord bless him! It was neither the first nor the last act of Christian kindness we have received at his hand. So building a camp-fire out of doors, we brought our ovens and skillets into use. That did pretty well until the rains began to descend upon us, and then for a sick wife to stand over a drowning fire was not exactly the thing. We had room in doors for a stove, but a small cooking-stove was worth at least one hundred dollars.

Happily for us in this emergence, the firm of Collins & Cushman, in San Francisco, presented us with a good new cooking-stove, just the thing we then most needed. I paid three dollars per joint for the necessary pipe, and five dollars for a common tin coffee-pot.

The question now was, "What shall we do at the end of the month?" Some said, as the Missionary Society had sent us there they would be bound to support us. I replied that the Missionary Society never had, and never could support a man at California rates; that my rent alone for a year would be about five thousand dollars, to say nothing of other expenses; that the society, moreover, was in debt, and that I never expected to draw on them for a dollar while in California. I said to the brethren that if nothing better opened I would take my ax and wedge, and go to the Redwoods, fifteen miles distant across the bay, and get out lumber for a house, and build it myself. They said I could not do it; but could suggest no other way of getting a house.

A brother who had located from the traveling ranks to try his fortunes in California, said: "Poor Brother Taylor will work himself sick, and that will end the matter. It had been better for him to come to California on his own hook as I did." I said that I had come in the order of Providence, and that I did not believe that God would allow my family to suffer for want of shelter.

I saw no other way, however, but to go to the Redwoods, and leave the result with the Lord. Alexander Hatler, a brother from Missouri, who, with his good wife, had emigrated to that land before gold was discovered, said he would go with me, and help me get out lumber. So on Tuesday, the 10th of October, we set sail for the Redwoods, in company with some of Father White's family, who had a shanty in the woods, where the old man and his sons spent much of their time, getting out and hauling lumber.

We landed where the town of San Antonia is now located. We then had five miles to walk, and climb a mountain, carrying our packs of blankets, provisions, and working tools. We reached the shanty a little after dark. Brother Hatler and I put our stock of provisions into the family mess, and were admitted as guests, with the privilege of wrapping in our own blankets, and sleeping on the ground, under the common shelter. After supper we listened to Father White's thrilling backwoods stories till bedtime; and then at the family altar we made the tall forests vocal with our song of praise.

The next morning Brother Hatler and I found a large log that some woodsman had abandoned, which we thought could be worked to good advantage. We drove all our wedges into it, but could not split it, so it took us till noon to chop our wedges out. A heavy rain then set in, which continued till the next morning.

On Thursday we worked till noon on another log. Being very large we had to bore it, and burst it open with powder; but it was too cross-grained for our purpose. We then selected a large tree, and chopped at it till dark. The next morning brought our giant of the forest to the ground; but, alas! we could not work it. It was difficult to find a tree with straight grain and easy to split; but the trees were so large, many of them measuring twelve feet in diameter, that when a good one was opened it yielded almost a yardful of lumber. But we did not succeed in getting the right tree.

On Friday P. M. we returned to the landing, so as to take the land breeze early on Saturday morning, and be in the city in time for the appointments of the Sabbath. We lay on the beach that night, in the open air, to gaze at the stars, listen to the howling of the coyotes, (a small species of wolf,) or the gabble of multiplied thousands of wild geese, and the quacking of wild ducks, or meditate, or sleep, as we felt inclined. I took my turn at each of these, especially the last.

The city brethren were not at all disappointed with the result of our trip to the woods. It was just as they expected; but I surprised them by telling them that I was not at all discouraged, and meant to try it again the next week.

That was my fourth Sabbath in the city, and the second to preach in our new chapel. It was crowded that day, and we had a memorable season. I made provision for my appointments on the following Sabbath, so as not to be under the necessity of returning from the woods for a fortnight. Brother Hatler could not leave his business to return with me to the Redwoods, so I had to depend on my own muscles and skill alone. That week I wrought very hard, and was a little scared one night, as the following extract from my journal will show:

"*Friday, October* 19, 1849.—We are here on the territory of grizzly bears and wild cats, which are frequently seen by the wood-choppers. I had some expectation of a visit from a grizzly last night. We butchered a calf in the evening, which we had purchased from a Spaniard, and had it in the shanty. I lay before the open door, and thought if bruin should come in to get some veal I would have the honor of his first salutation. But, thought I, the God who saved me from the dangers of the deep will surely keep the bears off me. With these reflections I fell into a sweet sleep.

"After midnight I was suddenly awakened by a noise outside the hut. I sprang up, saying to myself, 'There's the bear, sure enough!' when in he came;

but, to my comfort, I found it one of the men of the shanty. Such are many of the dreadful bears we encounter in this life."

On Friday, the 19th of October, I went to a woodman's tent, to sharpen my draw-knife, and found there a man, by the name of Haley, very far gone with diarrhea. Soon as I mentioned the subject of religion to him he burst into tears, and cried like a child. He told me that he had once enjoyed religion, and had been a member of the Baptist Church; but, in his wanderings in these Western wilds, he had got off the track, and lost his religion. I prayed with him, and he promised to give his heart, there and then, to God. When I called to see him the next day I found him rejoicing in the love of Jesus.

"O, I'm so glad," said he, "that you called in yesterday to see me! I had thought of sending for you, but I felt so guilty I could not have the courage to do so; but now I feel that God, for the sake of Jesus, has pardoned all my sins. My soul is happy: I am not afraid to die now."

Poor fellow! I expected him to die within a few days, but afterward learned that he recovered.

Three years after this, one night, at the close of meeting in the Bethel, in San Francisco, a man introduced himself to me, and asked me if I remembered praying with a dying man in the Redwoods, in 1849.

I replied: "Yes, sir, I do."

Said he: "I am that man; and my soul is still happy in God."

I believe this was the first man I was permitted to lead to Jesus in California. A little of my Redwood experience is noted in my journal of Saturday, October 20, as follows:

"I experience a good degree of the love of God in my soul this evening; but I should feel better could I spend the approaching Sabbath at some point more important. O that my house were built, and my family settled, that I might be wholly given up to the great work of my mission. I feel, however, that I am working now, in this Redwood, for the Missionary Society and the Church, and that, by the labor of a few weeks, I can live without another draft on the funds of the society. O my Master, help me in my work of avoiding expense to the Missionary Board, and in my work of saving sinners in California!"

It may not be amiss here to insert another bit of experience from my journal:

"*Sunday morning, October* 21, 1849.—For retirement and meditation I have strolled out to the top of a high hill. The sky is clear as crystal, and the sun is shining with a California radiance, unknown in other lands. O this is a delightful Sabbath, and I have just been waking the echoes of the wilderness with that sweet song:

'Welcome sweet day of rest,
That saw the Lord arise,' etc.

Looking eastward I see a dense forest of huge redwood timber; doubtless the veritable cedars of Lebanon. West and north, hills and mountains stretch to the uttermost line of the ken of vision, and the scene, in its barrenness and sterility of appearance, is only relieved here and there by a small oasis, and by the herds of cattle feeding on the dry grass. Southward the whole valley, for fifty miles, is filled with fog. It looks as though a firmament of white broken clouds had dropped from the heavens, and settled over the whole region of the Bay of San Francisco and its adjacent vales. Here I stand on a summit above the clouds. Many walk beneath those clouds in comparative darkness, while I bathe in the brightest sunlight. It is well for every lover of Jesus to rise above the world, and dwell on the Mount of Holiness, walking 'in the light as God is in the light.'

"A little to my right are two graves. There sleep the dust and buried hopes of two California adventurers. Whence were they? What their names? Who are their parents? Do they yet live to inquire after their sons in the far West? What was the character of these sons? What the circumstances of their death? Where now are their souls? These are questions which arise in my mind, but no voice responds. This is a lonely, solemn place. Its loneliness is increased by the numerous vultures which are floating through the air over my head, and the hoarse croaking of the raven. 'O my Master, bless me, and keep me wholly thine! My dear sick wife and babes, I leave in thy hands!'"

I may here add that I preached that Sunday under the shade of a large redwood tree to twenty-five woodsmen. One of my hearers, a man of forty-five years, heard preaching that day for the last time. He soon afterward took suddenly ill, and died, and was added to the two lonely strangers on the neighboring hill. The ensuing week I finished my work in the woods. My scantling, which I bought in a rough state, split out like fence rails, I hewed to the square with my broadax. I got my joists from a man who had a saw-pit. I made three thousand shingles, and gave them for twenty-four joists, seventeen feet long. I bought rough clapboards six feet long, and shaved them down with my draw-knife for weather-boarding; and thus got in the woods all the materials for a two-story house sixteen by twenty-six feet, except flooring, doors, and windows. I bought the doors from a friend at a reduced price, eleven dollars per door. The windows one dollar per light, ten by twelve inches. It cost me twenty-five dollars per thousand feet to get my lumber hauled to the landing, and the regular price of freight from there to the city was forty dollars per thousand feet; but by hiring a boat and working myself, I got it done for less than half that price.

After digging a foundation on the church lot, rear of the chapel, and getting my lumber ready for building a parsonage, I was led to change my choice of location by the following facts, as noted from my journal:

"*Friday, October* 26.—I have all along designed building a parsonage on the church lot, thinking that when the brethren should get through with the chapel debt, they might refund to me the actual cash I expend in the building. But I find that, though I shall save more than half the cash cost of such a house by my own labor, it will nevertheless cost more money than the brethren will feel able to pay, and much more probably than they would have to pay two years hence for a house that will suit them much better for a parsonage.* Moreover, if I build on the church lot, we shall have to carry all the water we use up a long, steep hill; or, if brought to us, it will cost us twelve cents per bucket. If, therefore, I can get a lot convenient to water, and build on my own account, and thereby save the society the enormous rents, or present rates of building a parsonage, I shall be doing the Church a good service in that regard,

* Brother Simonds built there three years afterward a better parsonage for less than half the cost of my house.

and may on the property save myself from heavy loss in the end."

In the mean time Brother Hatler bought a lot, and built a house for himself and family on Jackson-street, above Powell, and proposed to me, if I would buy the next lot adjoining and build, and be his neighbor, he would dig a good well at our door, and would advance me the money to pay for my lot, and let me refund it when I could, without interest. So I bought a lot next door to Brother Hatler, twenty-three by one hundred and thirty-seven and a half feet, for twelve hundred and fifty dollars.

Brother Hatler, being a carpenter, gave me instruction and some help in building my house. I hired a few carpenters to hasten the business, as the wet season was upon us, till I got the house under roof. I paid my carpenters twelve dollars a day, and while they were at work for me, the men of their craft in the city struck for higher wages, sixteen dollars a day, threatening a penalty, which I need not mention, on any carpenter who should work for less; so I had to come up to the figures of sixteen dollars per day. So soon, however, as I got my house under roof, I dismissed my men, and did the rest of the work with my own hands, except occasionally a brother passing along would give me a few hours' work. Clarkson Dye, now proprietor of the Tremont House, New-York, put up my stairs. Treat Clark gave me a day or two; but I wrought daily from dawn till dark myself till it was finished. While digging the foundation I found the stakes of the original Methodist blue-tent. It happened that I was building on the very spot where Father White had pitched his blue-tent in which he held the first class-meetings in the spring of 1849. So we seemed to be on consecrated ground. If it had not been before, it certainly was afterward, by the glorious class-meetings and bright conversions in our pioneer house.

In six weeks from the time we moved into Captain Webb's house we moved into our own, and thus avoided paying one cent of rent. I had two rooms up stairs to rent, to help pay for the building, and had one fitted up for strangers, and especially for preachers, if we ever should be favored with the company of any. We had just got it furnished when Rev. J. Doane and his wife, missionaries for Oregon, arrived, and rejoiced to find so good a "prophet's room" in San Francisco. But we waited more than a year before the first recruit of missionaries for California arrived.

A forcible entry was made into my house as soon as I got it under roof, by an immense immigration from all climes of the rat tribe. Their multitude almost equaled that of the frogs of Egypt, and they were everywhere, in "bed-chambers," "ovens," and "kneading troughs." We could scarcely walk the

A STREET SCENE ON A RAINY NIGHT.

streets at night without being brought into contact with them. I brought one to an untimely end one night by accidentally setting my foot on it in the street. I have seen them swimming in the bay, from ship to ship, and when pursued they would dive and swim under water like minks. Mrs. Taylor had a beautiful counterpane, presented to her by friends in Baltimore, which she laid away carefully for safe keeping. One night, as she was taking it up for examination, she found it cut full of holes, and out sprang two China rats, white as cotton, with bright colored eyes surrounded by a streak of red. Having never seen any of that color before, their appearance produced quite a sensation in the family; we succeeded in capturing one of them, and having heard that if a singed rat were turned into a nest of rats they would all leave the house, we tried the experiment on our China fellow. We gave his white coat a good singeing, not, however, so as to hurt his feelings, and let him go. I really thought that the unsightly appearance of his ratship, and the smell of fire he bore away with him, would be a caution to all the family. His China friends took the hint and left, but the huge gray and black rats stood their ground and held possession of the premises. Those who could build rat-proof houses were highly favored among men. I used to see this notice on the door of a little house built over a well: "Shut the door and keep the rats out of the well, the *nasty things.*" But long ago the rats, rogues, and gamblers have been reduced to great straits in that city, and are now seen but seldom.

In addition to building materials for our house, I brought from the woods material to fence in the back part of our lot for a garden. But says one, "Are you a carpenter and gardener too?" I am neither one nor the other, but I had faith in God, and lacked not confidence in my own muscles, and in my skill to direct them in building, digging, and doing whatever else was necessary for a living in the land to which we had been sent to labor for God. Our garden flourished so that in a few weeks from the commencement of the rains in October, we had turnips, greens, and lettuce in abundance, a luxury enjoyed, I believe, by but one other family in the city. A restaurant keeper, passing by our garden one day, said to Mrs. Taylor: "I would like to buy some of your greens, madam; what do you ask for them?" "We have not offered any for sale," she replied, "but as we have more than we need, you can have some at your own price." Said he, "I'll give you ten dollars for a water-pail full." He took them, paid the money, and in a few days returned for more. Mrs. Taylor filled his pail again, and told him she would not take ten dollars for them, but would be well satisfied with eight. She then asked him how he could afford to pay such prices? "Well," said he, "I boil the greens slightly, with a little bacon, and get for them, when ready for use, fifty cents a fork. I make a very good profit on them."

We were now pretty well fixed, but Mrs. Taylor thought our little home would look more homelike if we could have a few chickens. So she applied to a neighbor lady who had a good stock of poultry, and the lady replied that she would be happy to accommodate her, and as she was the missionary's wife, she might have them at a reduced price.

"How much, Mrs. C., will you charge me for a rooster and two hens?"

"You can have the three, madam," replied Mrs. C., "for eighteen dollars."

Mrs. Taylor paid the price demanded, and brought home the fowls. I built a house for their accommodation, and put a lock on it to secure them at night, but some hungry fellow came along a few nights afterward, pulled a board off the rear end of the house, and carried away the cock and one of the hens, and we saw them no more. The remaining hen soon paid for herself in eggs.

Having to buy milk for our little Oceana, we got a supply daily from a neighbor, at the low rate of one dollar per quart. One dollar and a quarter per quart was the selling price, but being missionaries we were specially favored. Our milkwoman did business also in the egg line, and offered us six dollars per dozen for all we had to spare. She gave us but six dollars, because she bought to sell again for nine dollars per dozen. So when it was not convenient for us to pay money for milk, we found a convenient currency in eggs, at fifty cents apiece.

In the course of human events our milkwoman moved away, and we bought for milk some kind of a chalk mixture that made our little girl sick; so I sent to Sacramento City, where good cows could be got cheap, and bought a cow for two hundred dollars, and then we had plenty of good milk of our own. Such was life in California in 1849.

I have gone thus into detail, not to exhibit mine as a peculiar case, for it was not so, but simply to illustrate California life. As for sufferings I had none. My labors in house building were simply a good acclimating process, which increased my physical power, and prepared me the more effectively to endure the ministerial toil to which I was called. As for comforts, I was better off than most of my neighbors. We had a comfortable home, while the great mass of our "city folks" lived in very inferior shanties and tents.

I have often gone out in the morning after a stormy night, and found whole rows of tents lying flat on the ground, and scattered in every direction by the merciless blasts of winter; and many of my brethren in the ministry, at a later day, suffered probably greater trials and hardships than I did at the beginning. The Lord bless and reward them, for he only knows how great and varied have been the trials of missionary life in California.

CHAPTER II.

MISSIONARY LIFE—CONTINUED.

When the organization of the "Oregon and California Mission Conference" was authorized by the General Conference of 1848, Rev. William Roberts, who had been sent as missionary to Oregon the year before, was appointed superintendent of the missionary work in both territories; a good appointment, for he is a capable, noble brother, and a faithful minister of the Gospel; but his services were in great demand in Oregon, and being fully committed to the work there, and having his family and home there, more than seven hundred miles distant from San Francisco, he was only able to render to California the semi-annual visit of a few weeks.

His first visit as superintendent was in the summer of 1849, during which he preached in San Francisco, Sacramento City, Coloma, and perhaps at other points. A friend, who heard him preach at Coloma, says that Rev. Mr. Damon, from the Sandwich Islands, preached that day in the same house, and a "hat collection" of one hundred and thirty dollars was raised, to be divided equally between the two preachers, to defray their traveling expenses. In the "hat" was found a twenty and a ten-dollar piece, carefully folded in paper, on which was written, "I design the twenty dollars for Mr. Roberts, because he fearlessly dealt out the truth against the gamblers. The ten dollars are for Mr. Damon." Signed by the leading gambler of the town.

Without casting the slightest reflection on Brother Damon, for I believe him to be a faithful man of God, I would remark that the conduct of the gambler is a good illustration of a prominent characteristic of Californians generally, however wicked; for while they will not endure low abuse, they want a man, and especially a minister of the Gospel, to speak out the whole truth fearlessly, boldly, and to make thorough work of whatever he undertakes.

I heard of a would-be preacher in California, who tried to become "all things to all men" in a sense that the great apostle would not approve. He fell in company with a fine-looking man, whom he took to be a gambler, and made himself very agreeable to him indeed, till finally the latter remarked:

"The old fogies at home would be horror-stricken to see a man of your cloth associating so familiarly with one of my profession."

"O," said the preacher, "I look upon your profession in a very different light from that of most ministers. California is a peculiar country; a country of chance in every department of business; and *games* of chance are about on a par with everything else, and gambling has been made honorable here by the many honorable men who have engaged in it."

"By Harry!" rejoined the other; "do you mean to insinuate that I am a gambler? If I were a gambler I wouldn't show myself in decent society. I belong to the *stage;* but I want you to understand that I'm no gambler," and, turning on his heel, he cut the acquaintance of his fawning friend.

The justly mortified preacher found that he had set his moral standard too low for California common sense, and quite undershot his mark.

I will in justice say, that I know of no *regular* missionary of any denomination in California who has acted the part of the preacher just referred to.

Brother Roberts on this trip secured from Captain Sutter the donation of a church lot in Sacramento City; and hearing that I was bringing with me, via Cape Horn, the frame of a church from Baltimore, he decided that it, on arrival, had better be shipped to Sacramento City, and he would, immediately on his return, have one for San Francisco, framed and shipped from Oregon.

Captain Gelson set apart for the Methodist Episcopal Church in San Francisco, a fifty vara lot, one hundred and thirty-seven and a half feet square, near the corner of Montgomery and Pine-streets; but "it was away over in the sand-hills, qnite out of town;" and the brethren bought, for two thousand dollars, the half of a fifty vara lot on Powell-street, on which to erect the forthcoming church. Captain Gelson then sold the said fifty vara lot for one thousand dollars, and subscribed that amount to the new church enterprise on Powell-street.

The church site on Powell-street was, like Mount Zion, "beautiful for situation;" the top of a high hill, above the town, commanding a grand view of the bay and surrounding country, and requiring nearly all who desired to worship there to say: "Let us go up to the house of the Lord." But the *going up* was so heavy a business that the location for a church was, for several years, very unfavorable indeed. A large number of families having since settled on that and on other hills still further west, it has become a very good location for a church.

The Gelson lot, however, which was twice as large, and was sold for half the price of this, was within less than four years in nearly the center of the city, and one of the best church sites in it, but could not be bought for less than thirty thousand dollars.

On this visit to California Brother Roberts brought with him his blankets, sleeping and traveling gear, and on his arrival bought and rigged up a mule, and thus traveled on "the foal of an ass" in primitive independent style, carrying a Bible in one hand and a good Colt's revolver in the other. The Bible he had occasion to use every day, the blankets every night, but happily for him and for all the hostile foes he encountered, the sight of the "fire-dog" was enough.

On his next visit, a few months later, he brought his blankets again; but we informed him that he need not untie them, as California had so risen in the scale of civilization, and had so advanced in internal improvements, that she could furnish at least one bed, blankets and all, for the ministers who might visit her shores. He ascertained that it was even so, and I saw no more of his blankets.

On my arrival in San Francisco I found the frame of the said church from Oregon up, and the floor laid; size, twenty-five by forty feet. There was as yet no regular board of trustees; but Brothers Troubody, Hatler, White, and others were earnestly at work "building a house for the Lord." They had paid eleven hundred dollars freight on the lumber from Oregon, and were paying the carpenters as the work proceeded, so that when the church was finished they owed nothing except the cost of the lumber in Oregon, which was nearly fifteen hundred dollars. Some months afterward, when Brother Roberts presented the lumber bill, they raised and paid over nearly five hundred dollars, and turned over to Brother

Roberts Captain Gelson's thousand dollar subscription.

This, the second Protestant, and first Methodist church built in California, was dedicated the third Sunday after my arrival, October 8th, 1849. I preached the dedication sermon to a crowded house, from: "The voice of him that crieth in the wilderness, Prepare ye the way of the Lord, make straight in the desert a highway for our God. Every valley shall be exalted, and every mountain and hill shall be made low, and the crooked shall be made straight, and the rough places plain. And the glory of the Lord shall be revealed, and all flesh shall see it together; for the mouth of the Lord hath spoken it." I was assisted in the dedicatory services by Rev. O. C. Wheeler, Baptist minister; Rev. Alfred Williams, Presbyterian; and Rev. T. Dwight Hunt, Congregationalist.

These were all the Protestant pastors in the city at that time, except Rev. Mr. Mines and Rev. Dr. Vermehr, who, though friendly enough in social life, did not, being Episcopal clergymen, give us an ecclesiastical fraternization. But the three brethren above named all extended to me a hearty welcome on my arrival, and afterward ever exhibited gentlemanly courtesy, and the good-will of a common Christian brotherhood.

In connection with our dedication service, we dedicated our little missionary girl to the Lord by baptism. Born on the ocean on our voyage round Cape Horn, we called her Oceana. The ordinance was administered by Rev. William H. Hatch. Brother Hatch had that year located from the New-England Conference, and became the chaplain of a large mining company which arrived in San Francisco in the fall of 1849, in the ship Araetus, Captain Wooley. They were going to dig a mint of gold, establish a colony, build a church; and Brother H., for his services as chaplain, was to share equally in the profits with those who were to dig the gold. It was a magnificent arrangement.

I met with this ship's company at Valparaiso, *en route* to California, and there, by the politeness of Brother Hatch, taking a peep through their telescope of manifest destiny, I saw the beautiful vision of their dreams. But soon after their arrival in California, as was invariably the case with large mining companies in those days, they disagreed with each other, disbanded, and every one took his own course.

Brother Hatch had made no calculation on going to manual labor. His prospects of success and usefulness were built alone on the unity and success of the company; but now it was all broken up, and he was left in the lurch, which was almost as shocking to his nervous system as to his bright hopes, and *lee-lurched* him so low in a spell of sickness, that for weeks it was very doubtful whether he ever would *right up* again. Poor brother, I really pitied him. There he was, nearly six thousand miles from his family, out of funds, out of health, but few friends, and they constantly engaged in looking out for themselves; no home, no employment, and expense of a mere subsistence enormous. The brother was in a bad case, and somehow, whenever an itinerant Methodist preacher locates, however pure his motives, and afterward gets into adversity, he shares in the sympathy of his friends about as largely as did Jonah when swallowed by the whale. To make the matter worse, the unhappy sufferer is very apt to join with his friends in reproaching himself. When Brother Hatch got able to work a little, he had, from necessity, to take the position of a waiter in the mechanic's boarding-house, from which some slanderer reported at home that he was selling rum. There was, however, no bar in the establishment, being simply an eating-house, and Brother Hatch was engaged in the very honorable business of washing dishes, setting table, etc. He afterward went to the mines, and I learned had good success in digging gold; and what was better, regained a higher degree of health than he had enjoyed for years before.

From an intimate personal acquaintance with Brother Hatch during most of his sojourn of a couple of years in California, I have to say of him, that however great his mistake in locating, I believe, through all his humiliating reverses and subsequent prosperity, he conducted himself as a Christian gentleman, and as a minister preached frequently, and always with faithfulness and acceptability. He is a good Gospel preacher, and immediately on his return to his family resumed his work as an itinerant in the New-England Conference.

Our congregations being too large for our little church, we made, in the early part of 1851, an addition to the rear end of it, twenty feet in depth by thirty-five in width, giving the house the form of the letter T. This enlargement cost about sixteen hundred dollars.

In 1854 the original church was sold and moved off the lot, and a fine wood edifice erected, fifty by eighty feet, at a cost of about fifteen thousand dollars.

The old church is now used as a dwelling on an adjoining lot.

The Baltimore California Chapel, though second in its erection by a few weeks, was the first Protestant church ever prepared for California use. It was framed in Baltimore by John W. Hogg, in February, 1849, having doors, windows, tin roof, and everything furnished, just ready, like the materials of Solomon's temple, for being put up.

The friends in Baltimore not only thus provided a

church, but paid all the freight on it to San Francisco. Whole amount contributed, eleven hundred and ninety-eight dollars and seventy-four cents. Of this North Baltimore Station paid four hundred and sixty-four dollars. The rest was made up in Light, Eutaw, Fayette, and Charles-street Churches, with a few private donations. The largest subscriptions was fifty dollars, by Durias Carter. It cost upward of five hundred dollars to freight this little chapel from San Francisco to Sacramento City, an amount exceeding the freight from Baltimore to San Francisco; but it was a godsend to the Sacramentans, for they greatly needed a church, and lumber there was four hundred dollars per thousand feet. Prior to the erection of the church they had preaching under an oak-tree, and sometimes in a blacksmith's shop.

Though the Methodists were the first Protestants to explore California as a missionary field, Rev. William Roberts and Rev. J. H. Wilbur, Methodist missionaries to Oregon, having as early as May, 1847, visited San Francisco, Monterey, and other points, and made earnest appeals to the Church on the importance of sending missionaries there immediately; and though the General Conference of the Methodist Episcopal Church, as early as May, 1848, authorized the organization of the "Oregon and California Mission Conference," and the appointment of two missionaries for California that year, still, in the order of time, we were considerably behind other denominations in occupying the field.

Rev. T. D. Hunt, who had for some time been in the service of the "American Board of Commissioners of Foreign Missions," arrived in San Francisco, from the Sandwich Islands, in October, 1848.

"Three days after his arrival he was formally invited by the prominent citizens of the place, of every religious persuasion, to reside among them, and act as chaplain of the town for one year, dating from November 1, 1848. A salary of two thousand five hundred dollars was voted at the public meeting as compensation for his services, and was promptly subscribed, and paid in quarterly installments. The school-house on the Plaza was appropriated by the town as the place of public worship, and services were at once held in it at eleven o'clock A.M., and half past seven P.M. of every Sabbath."

Acting thus as chaplain for the town, Mr. Hunt did not organize a Church until July, 1849, when he organized the "First Congregational Church." Their first house of worship, size about twenty-four by forty feet, was built on the corner of Jackson and Virginia streets, and was dedicated February 10, 1850; four months after the dedication of our chapel on Powell-street. They subsequently built a brick church on the corner of California and Dupont streets, where they now have a flourishing society and Sunday school, under the pastoral care of Rev. Mr. Lacy, Mr. Hunt having returned to the State of New-York.

The steamship California, which arrived in San Francisco, February 28, 1849, brought four missionaries from New-York, namely, Rev. O. C. Wheeler, a Baptist, Rev. S. Woodbridge, an Old School Presbyterian, Rev. J. W. Douglass, and Rev. S. H. Willey, both New School Presbyterians.

Rev. O. C. WHEELER immediately commenced operations in San Francisco, and on June 24, 1849, organized the "First Baptist Church." They soon afterward built a church on Washington-street, between Dupont and Stockton streets, size about thirty by fifty feet, which was the first Protestant church built in California. They have since erected a brick edifice on the same site, in which Rev. B. Brierly officiates as pastor, Rev. Mr. Wheeler having gone to Sacramento City.

Rev. S. WOODBRIDGE established a Church in Benicia, where he still resides as pastor. He was chaplain of the California Legislature, during the sojourn of that *migratory institution* in Benicia; for the location of the State Legislature was, for several years, one among the ten thousand contingences of California life. San José was first fixed by law as the capital of the state. Subsequently General M. G.

Vallejo, a wealthy Castilian, himself one of the legislators, living north of the Bay of San Francisco, offered, I believe, nearly half a million of dollars for public buildings, etc., if they would locate the capital in a city bearing his name, to be laid out, and built on the shore of "Napa Straits," opposite Mare Island, where the Pacific Navy Yard is now located. His proposition was accepted, and the next session of the Legislature appointed to be held in the new city that was to spring up during the year. The magnificent paper "City of Vallejo" was forthwith surveyed and plotted, containing beautiful parks, and all the modern improvements, and a rare opportunity for investment afforded to everybody who wished to be property holders in the great metropolis of the state.

The next year, when the law-makers assembled in the new capital, they were not exactly satisfied with the new State House, nor the accomodations afforded by the town for their comfort; in short, they believed that the general had not fulfilled his contract with them, and about arrived at the conclusion that his offer was predicated on the sale of city property, which had not been so productive as was anticipated, and they did not feel like waiting till the money could be made in that way.

Benicia, a rival town seven miles distant from Vallejo, then put in a bid for the job of accommodating that honorable body, and through some *log-rolling* process succeeded. Benicia was then the permanent capital of the state, and her real estate commanded good prices. San José, however, still claimed by constitutional right to be the capital; but nobody could answer the simple question, "Which is the capital of California?" After a tremendous amount of heaving on the political windlass, the government anchors were weighed, and the Legislature permanently moored in Sacramento City. Land speculators made a capital thing out of these removals of the capitol; but the expense to the state was enormous, beyond my present means of computation, and many a poor fellow who wanted a home in the State capital was badly taken in.

Rev. J. W. Douglass preached a year or two in San José, and afterward became editor and publisher of "The Pacific," a religious paper published in San Francisco. Mr. Douglass subsequently returned to New-York, and the said paper is now edited by Rev. Mr. Brayton.

Rev. S. H. Willey landed at Monterey, and remained there a year and a half. During his stay there the convention that framed the State Constitution met in Monterey, and Mr. Willey officiated as chaplain. He subsequently went to San Francisco, and organized the "The Second Presbyterian Church" in that city, of which he is still pastor.

Rev. Albert Williams arrived in San Francisco, in the steamship Oregon, April 1, 1849. After preaching a few times in the public school-house on the Plaza, he organized, on the 20th of May, the "First Presbyterian Church," composed at that time of six members. On the west side of Dupont-street, between Pacific-street and Broadway, they pitched a large tent, "which had been the marquee of a military company in Boston, and in it during the remainder of the dry season of 1849 they statedly held their meetings. It was plainly but neatly furnished with matting, pulpit, seats, and seraphine, and afforded accommodations for about two hundred persons." Mr. Williams also taught a small school in this tent. Their first church was built on Stockton-street, near the corner of Broadway, and was dedicated on the 19th of January, 1851. The materials had been purchased and framed by the liberality of friends in New-York, so the society in San Francisco had to pay nothing on the materials, except the freight from New-York, the respectable little item of three thousand dollars; and putting up and finishing the church cost ten thousand dollars more. It was of the early Gothic style of architecture, thirty-five feet wide by seventy-five feet in depth, and would seat eight hundred persons. So Mr. Williams, after waiting more than a year and a half, had now the best church in the state, and a good congregation. They, however, enjoyed their fine house but five months, when the sixth great San Francisco fire laid it in ashes. By the 12th of October, 1851, they had another, though a very plain one, ready for use on the same site, which still stands, and is now occupied by the same society under the pastoral care of Rev. Dr Anderson, Mr. Williams having returned to the East.

Rev. J. A. Benton, Congregationalist, arrived in the summer of 1849, and organized a church in Sacramento City, of which he is still the pastor.

Rev. F. S. Mines, an Episcopal clergyman, also arrived in the summer of 1849, and organized "Trinity Church," the first of his denomination in California. They built a small chapel next door north of the Methodist chapel on Powell-street, which was ready for use about January 1st, 1850. They afterward sold out to the Rev. Mr. Prevaux, Baptist minister, for an academy, which he successfully established, and built of corrugated iron a more commodious church on Pine-street, between Montgomery and Kearney-streets.

Mr. Mines died in 1852, the only clergyman who has ever deceased in that city. Rev. Dr. Wyatt is his successor.

Rev. Dr. Vermehr, also an Episcopal clergyman, arrived, *via* Cape Horn, a few days before I did, in September, 1849. He organized "Grace Parish" in April, 1850. "Grace Chapel" was opened for worship on December 30th, 1849, on Powell-street, about one square north of "Trinity Church." It was superseded by a commodious wood edifice near the same site, which was opened in July, 1851. Dr. Vermehr afterward took charge of a school in Sonora, and was succeeded by Bishop Kip.

Of these pioneer missionaries, the two Episcopal clergymen named, and the Rev. Messrs. Hunt, Wheeler, and Williams, were, as before stated, the only pastors established in San Francisco on my arrival; and with the two exceptions before mentioned, they received me with a cordial greeting as a co-laborer with them in the great work of evangelization in California. I know not that a discordant note was ever struck to disturb the harmony of our mutual friendly relations. As evidence of the fraternal feelings existing between us, we all dedicated our respective churches at twelve M., to afford the other congregations opportunity to get through with their regular morning services in time for the people to attend, and the ministers to participate in the dedicatory services. We also in those days had a ministers' meeting every Monday morning, where we prayed for each other, and for our respective charges, and exchanged words of mutual comfort and encouragement. We also discussed questions of general interest, and projected plans for promoting our common cause in California; for example, the organization of a "Strangers' Friend Society." The winter of 1849–50 was a very severe one for that climate, and especially so because the people were but very poorly provided with shelter to protect them from the heavy rainstorms. Provisions, too, were scarce, and prices enormously high; many, too, were without money, and friendless; consequently there was a vast amount of suffering and sickness, of which many died.

For the relief of destitute and sick strangers, the "Strangers' Friend Society" was organized in our church in Powell-street, about February 1st, 1850. Brothers Hunt, Wheeler, and Williams, with their congregations, all took an active part in this society, and it was the means of affording temporary relief to many sufferers. The society was not continued beyond the emergences of that winter; but another important movement grew out of it, which, if it had been successful in the accomplishment of its ends, would have resulted in great good to the city, and to thousands of sick strangers.

The principle of farming out the care of the sick to the lowest bidder, on which the city fathers were acting, was deplored by reflecting men as a great evil. The city was then paying five dollars per day for the care of each charity patient. The physician's honesty and sympathy might lead him to give to each patient five dollars' worth of attention, or his cupidity might restrict him to one dollar's worth of care to each patient, and cause the other four dollars to go into his own pocket. Such was thought by many to be too great a temptation to set before even an honest California doctor.

At a public meeting of "The Strangers' Friend Society," at the Baptist Church, on the 19th of February, 1850, a committee was appointed to draft and present a memorial to the City Council, praying for the erection by the city of a charity hospital. The committee consisted of the Revs. Wheeler, Hunt, Williams, and J. B. Bond, E. Townsend, Dr. Logan, and myself. The committee, after various meetings, prepared their memorial, to which was appended a plan illustrating the character of the contemplated hospital, and a constitution for its government, all of which were duly presented to the City Council. The city fathers seemed well pleased with our suggestions and plans, and said it would be just the thing needed if they had the money to carry it into effect; but, for want of funds, they respectfully declined to act. They, however, continued to pay out from four hundred to six hundred dollars per day for the care of the sick, even at the reduced rate of four dollars per day each patient. It was not many months until a debt of sixty-four thousand dollars hung over the city for the care of her sick strangers, for the recovery of which suit was instituted and a judgment given against the city, under which at least two million dollars' worth of city property was sacrificed; enough to have built half a dozen charity hospitals, and to have supported them by endowment for fifty years. But though our memorial was not honored by the City Council, it had a manifestly good effect on the management of the city hospital, by calling general attention to the subject of hospital abuses. The fears of those concerned in it were excited, their movements were watched more closely by their employers and by the public generally, and the sick consequently received better attention.

Another work in which we had hearty concert of action, was the organization of the Bible Society, of which the "Annals of San Francisco," a book full of valuable historical matter, published by Appleton & Co., New-York, has the following notice:

"On October 30th, 1849, a meeting of citizens friendly to the formation of a 'Bible Society,' was held in the Methodist Episcopal Church in Powell-street, at which Rev. T. Dwight Hunt presided, and Mr. Frederic Billings acted as secretary. Addresses were delivered by F. Buel, agent of the 'American Bible Society,' Messrs. F. Billings, and W. W. Caldwell; and on motion of Mr. William R. Wardsworth, the 'San Francisco Bible Society,' auxiliary to the 'American Bible Society,' was organized, a constitution adopted, and the following officers chosen, whom we recognize as the early laborers on this field, and who, with characteristic zeal, frankly joined hands, irrespective of sect or denomination: President, John M. Findley; vice-presidents, Rev. Dr. Ver Mehr, Rev. Albert Williams, and Rev. William Taylor; treasurer, W. W. Caldwell; secretary, Frederic Buel. Since its organization the society has been steadily engaged in its appropriate work of supplying the Scriptures to the citizens of the state, and has issued from its depository about ten thousand volumes, [1854,] in the different languages spoken in the state and adjacent territories, the majority by sale, and the remainder by donation to those unable to purchase. This institution has ably commended itself to the spirit of catholic Christianity by the universal circulation of that book within which its doctrines are comprehended. Other societies, for the same purpose, established in the interior, have materially aided this object.

"The depository of the society was destroyed by fire on the morning of the 26th of April, 1853; in place of which a new fire-proof brick building has been erected on the lot belonging to the society, No. 376 Stockton-street, between Union and Green-streets.

"The officers for 1854 are: President, Hon. D. O. Shattuck; vice-presidents, Rev. B. Brierly, Rev. M. C. Briggs, and Rev. S. H. Willey; secretary,

F. Buel; treasurer, E. P. Flint; executive committee, Colonel D. S. Turner, Major A. B. Eaton, Nathaniel Gray, George Wydoff, and R. P. Spier."

When Colonel M'Kee, one of the Indian agents appointed by the government at Washington to treat with the California Indians, was about to enter upon the discharge of his duties, he came to our ministers' meeting to consult them as to the best mode of reaching and civilizing the red men of the Pacific. We discussed the subject at large, and all concurred in the views of the colonel, namely: to colonize them on reservations, and place them under competent tutors, appointed by government, who should teach them husbandry and mechanism, and protect them against the rum-selling, extortionary, peddling fraternity of mean white men, who had been such a curse to all the Indian tribes of the East; and then, as soon as practicable, employ teachers to teach them science, and then missionaries to teach them salvation.

Such was, in substance, the plan there submitted and concurred in, and we all prayed over it, and committed it to the care of the red man's God and ours.

The plan has met with much opposition from three classes. First, from the Indian exterminators, who maintain that nothing can be done successfully to elevate, or long to perpetuate the red race; that while they exist they will ever be a treacherous and troublesome foe, and therefore the sooner they are all killed off the better. Second, from those who are jealous of the Indian's claim to the little tracts of land embraced in the reservations; and, third, from those who disapprove of government interference with the Indian's wild mode of living and native liberty.

Some of the last named class urge their objections no doubt from honest motives, but others from selfishness, because the plan, if properly executed, will debar them from their favorite mode of taming and civilizing the Indians, namely, by selling them rum, and robbing them of their furs or their gold dust.

But the colonization plan, notwithstanding all opposition, has, for the time it has been in operation, been successful beyond all precedent in Indian history.

In October, 1856, I got the following statistics in San Francisco, in the office of Col. T. J. Henly, superintendent of Indian affairs in California:

"The number of Indians now collected and residing on reservations is, at

Klamath	2,500
Nome Lackee	2,000
Mendocino	500
Fresno	900

Tejon	700
Nome Cult Valley, attached to Nome Lackee	3,000
King's River, attached to Fresno	400

"Making in all ten thousand. The number of Indians not connected with the reservations cannot be correctly estimated. The following statement is made up from the most reliable information I have been able to obtain:

On and attached to reservations, as above	10,000
In San Diego and San Barnardino Counties	8,000
Los Angelos, Santa Barbara, San Luis Obispo, Monterey, Santa Clara, and Santa Cruz Counties	2,000
Tulara and Mariposa	2,500
Tuolumne, Calaveras, San Joaquin, Alameda, and Contra Costa Counties	4,100
Sacramento, Eldorado, and Placer Counties	4,500
Sutter, Yuba, Nevada, and Sierra Counties	3,500
Butte, Shasta, and Siskiyou Counties	5,500
Klamath, Humboldt, and Trinity Counties	6,500
Mendocino, Colusi, Yolo, Napa, Sonoma, and Marin Counties	1,500

"Making the total number of Indians within this superintendence sixty-one thousand six hundred."

I learn that during the year 1857 another thousand Indians have been gathered in, and settled on the reservations. To illustrate the practical operation of this plan of colonization I here insert the following testimony concerning the Nome Lackee Reservation, from the official report of Mr. Charles E. Fisher, the assessor for Tehama County:

"I cannot close this report without speaking of the healthy and flourishing condition of Nome Lackee Reservation, which is situated twenty miles west of the Sacramento River, at the foot of the Coast Cange. Under the management of V. E. Geiger, it is in a more flourishing condition than ever before. Mr. Geiger is much beloved by the Indians, and keeps them under the strictest discipline; but still they are contented and happy. Between thirty and forty thousand bushels of grain were raised on the reservation this year, the work being all done by the Indians. Under the management of Mr. Geiger it will be but a short time till all the Indians in the northern part of California will be safely settled on the reserve."

I am sorry to say that the plan, so far as it relates to schools, and the preaching of the Gospel among the Indians on the reservations, has not as yet been carried into effect. I hope it will be very soon; for, however dull the parents may be, the children are bright, and capable of elevation. O how my heart has bled for them, as I have witnessed their sports, and listened to their merry shouts, as they skipped over the hills! I loved them as myself, being my brethren; and longed to see them enjoy my privileges of enlightenment and salvation.

CHAPTER III.

MISSIONARY LIFE — CONTINUED.

As we before stated, Rev. William Roberts organized a small class in San Francisco, in the summer of 1847, which was reorganized in the spring of 1849, by Brother Asa White.

The first quarterly meeting in California was held in our chapel on Powell-street. It commenced by the organization of a quarterly conference, on Saturday night, December 2, 1849. John Troubody, Alexander Hatler, and Willet M'Cord were elected stewards. Resolutions were passed, expressing thanks to the Missionary Board for sending them a missionary, and pledging themselves for his support, beyond the appropriation they had already made. The said new board of stewards fixed my salary and table expenses at two thousand dollars per year, including the missionary appropriation of seven hundred and fifty dollars, I finding and furnishing my own house.

On the Sunday of our quarterly meeting Rev. J. Doane, missionary, *en route* to Oregon, preached at eleven o'clock A. M. That morning I announced that I would preach at three o'clock P. M, on the Plaza. It was a startling announcement, which greatly excited the fears of some of the brethren; for nearly all the gamblers in the city were located round the Plaza, in the best houses the city afforded.

An idea of the prestige of the gambling fraternity, and the magnificence of their saloons in those days, may be obtained from the accompanying cut, representing, to the life, the interior of the El Dorado, a large gambling-house, at the northeast corner of the Plaza. The tables, loaded with gold and silver, you cannot see for the multitude; but in the rear end of the saloon you see, elevated on a stage, a band of the best musicians the country could furnish, sending forth their melody in such sweetness and variety as to crowd the house, and hold in admiration the promiscuous masses in the streets. I have heard them sing and play, "Home, sweet, sweet home," till homeless wanderers, by hundreds, would stand entranced, seeming to live for a time in the embrace of loved ones, surrounded by all the sweet associations of the past. Alas! it was but the song of the siren.

On the right may be seen the beautifully ornamented bar, with splendid mirrors in the rear, around which many a jolly circle of hopeful young prodigals drank to each other's health the deadly draught.

INTERIOR OF THE EL DORADO.

Such places were crowded, especially on Sunday, with men of all nations, the most daring and reckless, perhaps, in the world; and such was their dominant influence, that when they shot a man dead, as they frequently did, there were no arrests, and nothing said, but that "C. B. was killed last night in the Parker House."

The brethren knew that if the gamblers should regard my attempt to preach on the Plaza, thrilling every one of their saloons with the echoes of an unwelcome Gospel, as an interference with their business, and should shoot me down, there would be no redress. It would simply be said, "The gamblers killed a Methodist preacher." At the appointed time I was on the Plaza, accompanied by Mrs. T. and a few friends. I got Mrs. T. a chair, and put her in care of Dr. B. Miller, and appropriated a carpenter's workbench, which stood in front of the largest gambling-saloon in the place, as my pulpit. At that moment Clarkson Dye, thinking I might need some protection against the rays of the burning sun, went across to Brown's Hotel, and asked for the loan of an umbrella to hold over the preacher. He was met with the reply: "I won't let my umbrella be used for such a purpose, but if I had some rotten eggs I'd give them to him." He had to pay nine dollars per dozen for eggs, and couldn't afford to throw them at the preacher.

Taking my stand on the work-bench I sang:

"Hear the royal proclamation,
The glad tidings of salvation,
Publishing to every creature,
To the ruin'd sons of nature.
Jesus reigns, he reigns victorious
Over heaven and earth most glorious,
Jesus reigns!

"See the royal banner flying,
Hear the heralds loudly crying,
Rebel sinner, royal favor
Now is offer'd by the Saviour.
Jesus reigns, etc.

"Hear, ye sons of wrath and ruin,
Who have wrought your own undoing;
Here is life, and free salvation,
Offer'd to the whole creation.
Jesus reigns, etc.

"'Twas for you that Jesus died,
For you he was crucified,
Conquer'd death, and rose to heaven,
Life eternal's through him given.
Jesus reigns, etc.

"Here is wine, and milk, and honey,
Come and purchase without money;
Mercy, like a flowing fountain,
Streaming from the holy mountain.
Jesus reigns, etc.

"For this love, let rocks and mountains,
Purling streams and crystal fountains,
Roaring thunders, lightning blazes
Shout the great Messiah's praises.
Jesus reigns, etc.

"Turn unto the Lord most holy,
Shun the paths of sin and folly;
Turn, or you are lost forever,
O now turn to God your Saviour!
Jesus reigns, etc."

By the time the song ended, I was surrounded by about one thousand men. Restless hundreds, always ready for the cry, "A whale! a whale!" or any other wonder under the sun, came running from every direction, and the gambling-houses were almost vacated.

I had crossed the Rubicon, and now came the tug of war. Said I, "Gentlemen, if our friends in the Atlantic states, with the views and feelings they entertained of California society when I left them, had heard that there was to be preaching this afternoon on Portsmouth Square, in San Francisco, they would have predicted disorder, confusion, and riot; but we who are here believe very differently. One thing is certain, there is no man who loves to see those stars and stripes floating on the breeze, (pointing to the waving flag of our Union,) and who loves the institutions fostered under them; in a word, there is no true

American but will observe order under the preaching of God's word anywhere, and maintain it if need be. We shall have order, gentlemen. Your favorite rule in arithmetic is the rule of 'loss and gain.' In your tedious voyage round the Horn, or your wearisome journey over the plains, or your hurried passage across the Isthmus, and during the few months of your sojourn in California, you have been figuring under this rule; losses and gains have constituted the theme of your thoughts and calculations. Now I wish most respectfully to submit to you a question under your favorite rule. I want you to employ all the mathematical power and skill you can command, and patiently work out the mighty problem. The question may be found in the twenty-sixth verse of the sixteenth chapter of our Lord's Gospel by St. Matthew. Shall I announce it? 'What is a man profited if he shall gain the whole world, and lose his own soul?'"

Every man present was a "true American" for that hour. Perfect order was observed, and profound attention given to every sentence of the sermon that followed. That was our first assault upon the enemy in the open field in San Francisco, and the commencement of a seven years' campaign, which is illustrated in my book on "Street Preaching in San Francisco." I preached in the chapel that evening to a crowded house, and four men presented themselves at the altar as seekers of salvation.

I preached every night during that week, and three persons professed to experience religion; the first revival meeting in California. The little society was greatly refreshed, and especially encouraged by the fact that God could and did convert sinners in that land of gold and crime, a thing almost as incredible, even among Christians, at that time in California as the doctrine of the resurrection among the Sadducees. We had, upon the whole, though minus a presiding elder, a good old-fashioned quarterly meeting, never to be forgotten.

During the fall of 1849 we had but one class, which met every Sunday at three o'clock P. M. It contained but about thirty members; the meetings, however, were swelled by a constant stream of immigrating Methodism, to an average attendance of sixty persons, and frequently numbering as high as ninety. We had but very few females, a lack we keenly felt; for the great man, Moses, could not get along well without a sister to help him; and the Great Prophet, of whom Moses was a type, needed Marys and Marthas, and Joannas, who stood by him, 'mid shame and scorn,' to the death, the last to listen to his dying groans, the first to hail his welcome rising, and bear the coronation tidings of the King of Glory to their poor, frightened, desponding brethren.

What could the great apostle to the Gentiles have done but for the help of Phebe, Priscilla, and others, of whom he says: "I entreat thee also, true yoke-fellow, help those women which labored with me in the Gospel, whose names are in the book of life." But there, in California, we had to do the best we could with the assistance of but very few sisters. I had one, thank the Lord, who stood by me in every battle; but in a class-meeting of ninety persons we could number only two or three ladies. Yet we had glorious meetings notwithstanding, for they all had mothers, wives, or sisters far away, whose influence followed them across the continent, and over oceans, and there, vibrating on every nerve, stirred the tender sensibilities of their souls, and caused them, on the utterance of that sweet but mighty word HOME, to weep like children. By a rapid association of kindred thoughts their minds were carried forward to the longed for meeting again with distant loved ones, and the possible doubt of not meeting them again on mortal shores, led them to the anticipation of the glorious meeting of friends on the shores of immortality, and the inseparable and unceasing friendships of a home in heaven. Their uplifted hands, streaming eyes, and joyous shouts told of their far-reaching hope and faith, which pierced through the darkness of death, and fixed their unclouded gaze on the glories of God's own home, and theirs.

Those class-meetings, composed of Christian adventurers from every land, were intellectual, social, and religious feasts, full of heaven and glory. I never expect to see any more exactly like them. In that infant society there were some noble men; I will here notice a few of them.

Asa White, now past the meridian of life, a hardy sun-tanned pioneer of the woods, was a man of good common sense, and very generous heart, a local preacher of moderate abilities, a good exhorter, full of fire. He had three married daughters with him at that time, who, with his good wife and two of his sons-in-law, were all zealous Methodists. They could have a good meeting any time, whether anybody else came or not. They were closely bound together as a family band, by mutual confidence and ardent affection, and could have made a fortune, and done a great deal of good in almost any place in California, had they settled down; but they had been pioneers all their lives, moving westward in the van of early emigration, and having reached the western limit of the continent, they spent their time in moving up and down the shore, now in Oregon, now in California, then again to Oregon, then back again to California, men, women, and children, all of the same mind, and all moving together. They seemed, by their constant migrations, to say: "O that we had a new continent of unbroken forests, unscathed by the axe of civilization, well stocked with Indians, panthers, wildcats, bear, deer, elk, raccoons, and opossums, that we might spend our days in crossing it, and entertain ourselves in shooting game, felling timber, building log cabins, and in surprising pioneer Methodist preachers with our backwoods refinement and extraordinary sympathy and kindness.

Alfred Love, the unconverted son-in-law in the family, came the nearest making a permanent settlement in California of any of them. He was a very kind-hearted fellow, a sincere friend to the cause of religion, and I often tried to persuade him to be reconciled to God. He admitted the truth of all I said, but still pursued his own course.

One day he went out into the mountains alone to take a hunt. In working his way through a chaperel thicket, he suddenly stumbled on a huge grizzly bear. The grizzly put after him at full speed. Alfred dropped his gun, and ran for life, but soon perceived by the cracking of the brush behind him, and the heavy footfall of old bruin, that he was rapidly gaining on him. His course led him across a deep ravine, in the bottom of which was a deep cut washed out by the winter torrents. He had no time to get round it, and in attempting to jump across the cut, his foot slipped, and down he fell to the bottom. As he struck, the terrors of death got hold of him, and he found trouble and sorrow. There was no hope in further effort, so he lay in motionless affright, expecting the grizzly to separate his joints within a minute. Happily for him the bear leaped the cut right over him, and went on his course, I suppose wondering what had become of his man. After the bear passed out of sight, Alfred crawled out, and made tracks in the opposite direction.

I heard him say afterward: "While I lay there every moment expecting the bear to jump on me, I was so sorry I had not taken Mr. Taylor's advice, and given my heart to the Lord, while I had opportunity; but I thought it was all over with me then."

John Troubody is by birth an Englishman, but crossed the water with his wife in early manhood. He lived a while in Pennsylvania; then in Missouri; and moved across the plains to California in 1847, or 1848. He appears to be a slow man in everything, but he steps so cautiously and constantly, that he always comes out about even with the fastest in every race. He has acquired a handsome property in California. A man of unbending religious integrity, a true friend of the Methodist Episcopal Church, and has never forgotten "the rock whence he was hewn, nor the hole of the pit whence he was digged." His wife was also a member of the Church, and their house may be set down, I think, as the first Methodist preacher's home in California.

6

WILLET M'CORD, from Sing Sing, New-York, was by no means a noisy Methodist. He always had on hand a dish of wit and pleasantry for the social circle, and was always in his place in the class-room and prayer-meeting.

L. F. BUDD was a remarkably simple-hearted, inoffensive, conscientious brother, of generous, refined feelings, and stern integrity. He had spent several years in Costa Rica, Central America, as commercial agent for some mercantile firm, and was instrumental in leading a wealthy coffee planter there to Christ. This planter corresponded regularly with Brother Budd in San Francisco. I used to read his letters with great interest. They were full of spirit and life, and earnest prayers for the redemption of the Central American states from the chains of sin and superstition. I am sorry I have forgotten the planter's name. Budd went from Costa Rica to California, in the employ of the same house; and in the palmiest days of San Francisco for money-making, gave his time to his employers at a small salary, fixed according to Eastern rates, till the term of his engagement expired. He then invested his earnings in a house, which was to let for several months before it was occupied, while he had applications for it almost every week. He always inquired:

"For what purpose do you wish to rent my house?"

"I want to keep a boarding-house and a bar."

To which he always replied, "I can't let my house for the sale of grog."

Finally a man, who greatly desired the house, tried to argue him out of his position. Said he: "Budd, I don't see why you should be so squeamish here in California; why, you are worse than the old fogies at home. The people will have liquor; somebody will supply the demand, at great profit, and I may as well do it and make money as anybody; and now I'll give you three hundred dollars per month for your house, and will take good care of it; and what does it matter to you what I use it for, if I return it in good order?"

Said Brother Budd, in reply: "My dear sir, the curse of God is hanging over this rum-traffic and all its abettors, and my policy is to stand from under."

He had no family, but being very anxious again to see his sisters and other kindred in the East, he wound up his business in 1853, and on his homeward passage sickened and died. He was a great admirer of the ocean. I have often heard him tell of the blessed seasons of communion with God he enjoyed in Costa Rica, as he strolled daily along the ocean-shore from sunset till dark in quiet meditation. When the sea shall give up her dead, L. F. Budd will beyond a doubt have a glorious resurrection.

Alexander Hatler, from Missouri, one of my earliest and best California friends, with a heart full of kindness, which felt that no sacrifice was too great for the altar of his friendship, was so unassuming and timid that he never did much in public religious exercises. But he was a man of unblemished moral character, and a liberal supporter of the Church. His wife is the exact counterpart of himself.

J. B. Bond, son of Dr. Thomas E. Bond, deceased, did not make a loud profession of religion, and yet he was foremost in every good work, distributing tracts, visiting the sick, attending class, praying in the prayer-meetings, and giving his money freely to the Church and the poor. We missed him greatly when he returned to New-York.

D. L. Ross, our "most excellent Theophilus," good humored and pious, a sincere lover of God and of Methodism, was one of the strongest pecuniary bulwarks of our Church enterprises in California. We hoped to have retained him and his amiable wife; but after a few years they weighed anchor, and returned to New-York. The Lord reward them here, and in the day of eternity give them a mansion in heaven.

R. P. Spier (I will not call him an old bachelor, for he is not so old but that there is still hope in his case) is as pure and conscientious, I believe, as was Joseph in Egypt; very cautious and correct in everything he does, though better qualified for "bookseller and stationer" than governor of Egypt. He went into a mercantile copartnership in Stockton, California, at one time, but when the other partners resolved to sell rum he promptly withdrew. He renders so much service in carrying out the details of the pastoral work, keeping the church-register in order, visiting delinquent and sick members, etc., that we sometimes call him Bishop Spier.

William Henry Codington, from Sing Sing, New-York, almost a beardless youth, opened a butcher-shop on Kearney-street. Sabbath-breaking was almost universal throughout the land, and I don't suppose that any other butcher had as yet dreamed of keeping the Sabbath in California; but young Codington hung up in a prominent place in his shop this sign: "This Market closed on Sundays." I know several butchers who were then considered very wealthy, doing a great business seven days in the week, who have since gone into insolvency, and some of them into an untimely grave, while Brother Codington has acquired a handsome property, married a good wife to help in its enjoyment, and grown up a man of God, and a pillar in the Church.

Robert Beeching, from New-York, had a hard time of it in crossing the plains. The first Sunday morning after his arrival in San Francisco he met me at the church door, apologized for his rough appearance and threadbare clothing, and told me of his sufferings and reverses on his way to the land of gold. Said he: "I've been accustomed to wear decent clothes in New-York, and I feel ashamed to go into church looking as I do; and yet I love Jesus, and want to be with his people."

I saw in him, at a glance, a man, a Christian, a gentleman, and, taking him by the hand, conducted him to the "highest seat in the synagogue." He being a fine musician, some gamblers offered him thirty dollars per night if he would play in their saloon. There he was, five thousand miles distant from his family, minus friends, money, and employment. By playing an instrument, which was his delight even at home, he could make thirty dollars every night; how quickly he might make his "pile," return to his family, and do good with his money. It was a well-circumstanced temptation, and he was almost led to a parley with the enemy.

That week, when he came to class at my house on Jackson-street, he related in the meeting the facts as above given, and said, "'Truly God is good to Israel, even to such as are of a clean heart. But as for me, my feet were almost gone; my steps had well nigh slipped; for I was envious at the foolish, when I saw the prosperity of the wicked.' I have thought, 'Verily I have cleansed my heart in vain, and washed my hands in innocency.' I have at least tried to serve God for many years; but in my great trials I seemed to be almost forsaken. 'Behold, these are the ungodly who prosper in the world; they increase in riches.' When I thought to know the reason of this, it was too painful for me; until I came to this sanctuary of God; now understand I their end. 'Surely they stand in slippery places, and shall be brought to desolation, and utterly consumed with terrors.' 'But thou, O my God, art my portion forever. Whom have I in heaven but thee, and there is none upon earth that I desire beside thee.'"

His tall, manly form, flowing tears, sweet commanding voice, all contributed to produce an effect in the class-room which I cannot describe. He then sang a triumphant song of Zion, which thrilled every heart.

Isaac Jones was a Welsh local preacher, and by trade a printer. He was employed in the office of the "Evening Picayune," and made a special agreement with the proprietor of that journal that he should never be called on to work on Sunday.

Some weeks afterward his employer said to him one Saturday night: "Jones, the steamer has just arrived, and we have so much new matter to set up that I want you to lend a hand with the boys, and set up a few thousand ems to-morrow."

"My dear sir," replied Jones, "I am willing to work till twelve o'clock to-night, and commence work again at one o'clock on Monday morning; but you know I told you in the commencement that it was against my principles to work on Sunday, and we made an agreement to that effect."

"O well, never mind, go on in your own way," said the proprietor.

A few weeks after his employer came in late one Saturday night, and said to him again: "Now, Jones, it's no use talking; you see what a quantity of matter we have to set up for the next issue, and a great deal of it must go in type to-morrow. It has to be done, and you may just as well help to do it as for the other boys to do it all. The fact is, I won't have a man about me unless he is willing to work at all times whenever he is needed."

"Well," said Jones, "I shall be very sorry to lose my situation, for it is very expensive living here, and I am dependent on the daily labor of my hands for the support of my family; but if my continuance in your office and my support depend upon my working on the Sabbath, I'll beg my bread from door to door, or if need be I'll starve in the streets rather than desecrate God's holy day."

After bustling round among the type-stands a while, the proprietor replied: "Well, Jones, you are a good workman and an honest fellow, and I don't want you to leave me." Jones's triumphant death, and that of his good wife, Mary, are noticed in my "Seven Years' Street Preaching in San Francisco," p. 353.

William Phillips and his son John were English hardware merchants, and true as steel.

I mention these "few names in Sardis, [California,] which have not defiled their garments," simply as specimen illustrations of a large class of sin-hating, God-fearing men in our first society in San Francisco, and of a noble band of martyr spirits to be found in perhaps all the early Church organizations of the country, of different denominations. In popular esteem in those days religion was at a large discount. There were no inducements to make a stalking-horse of religion; hence, hypocrites and milk-and-water Christians stood aloof. Asa White and Colonel Allen from Kentucky, Robert Kellan, M. E. Willing, Calvin Lathrop, and James M'Gowan were our early local preachers in San Francisco. Our early class-leaders were Richard T. Hoeg, Horace Hoag, and J. W. Bones. William Gafney, now of the California Conference, and H. Hoag were exhorters.

Our second class in the Powell-street Charge was organized about January, 1850, and met every Tuesday evening at my house in Jackson-street. We had glorious meetings there, in which souls were occasionally converted to God. A small Sunday school was organized in our church in the fall of 1849, of which Robert Kellan was superintendent. It was a weak and delicate plant in Zion, but we watered and cultivated it, and it lived and grew, and is now quite a tree, bearing fruit to the glory of God. As was before mentioned, Rev. William Roberts, missionary, *en route* to Oregon, organized a small Sunday school in San Francisco in 1847, appointing J. H. Merrill superintendent. I have before me an original letter from Roberts to Merrill in regard to it, which, as a matter of history, I will here insert:

"MONTEREY, *May* 27, 1847.

"DEAR SIR:—I hereby send to you the library of primary Sunday-school books, of which I spoke when at San Francisco. They were found yesterday, and the captain of the Commodore Shubrick, I expect, will bring them to you without charge. There are one hundred and three volumes of books, one dozen cards, and one dozen catechisms, and also one register or receiving-book. These books are the property of the Sunday School Union of the Methodist Episcopal Church, and I place them in your hands for the use of the school under your care, with the hope that God's blessing may rest upon this effort to bless the youth of the land.

"I am yours respectfully,

"WILLIAM ROBERTS."

That Sunday school, numbering about twenty scholars, was kept up, as Mr. Merrill informed me, through the summer of 1847, soon after which gold was discovered, which caused a general stampede of both parents and children. I found the said Sunday-school library in care of Brother White on my arrival, and we appropriated it to the use of the school organized in 1849, as above described. The first "watch-night meeting" ever held in California came off in our Powell-street Church, at the closing of that eventful year, 1849. I extract the following from my journal in regard to it:

"*January* 1, 1850.—On last evening I preached in our chapel to about thirty persons, and held a watch-meeting. Though our meeting was not large, it was an occasion of great interest. After sermon, from the text, "What shall I render unto the Lord for all his benefits toward me? I will take the cup of salvation, and call upon the name of the Lord. I will pay my vows unto the Lord now in the presence of all his people," we occupied some time in the relation of Christian experience. A majority of all present spoke of the benefits they had received at the hands of God during the past year, and especially while encountering the dangers of the deep or of the desert. The exercises were concluded as the new year was being ushered in, by solemnly singing on our knees the covenant hymn:

"Come, let us use the grace Divine,
And all, with one accord,
In a perpetual covenant join
Ourselves to Christ the Lord," etc.

HYMN 1054, Methodist Hymn Book.

About this time the "Methodist Company," in the ship Arkansas, Captain Shepherd, arrived. According to their advertisement in New-York, the company was to be composed entirely of Methodists, and many joined it with that understanding, thinking it the rarest chance that ever was to get to California without being brought into contact with the wicked rabble that mixed in with promiscuous companies. But when they got out to sea and gathered the flock together, they soon found that the goats outnumbered the sheep. The voyage, socially and morally, was by no means a pleasant one; and I have no doubt that many of them adopted St. Paul's conclusion: that to be freed "altogether" from "fornicators, covetous, extortioners, or idolaters," "then must ye needs go out of the world." The night of their arrival in the port of San Francisco, before they could land, a heavy gale caught their ship, which dragged her anchors, and was carried by the violence of the storm till she struck Bird Island. There they were in midnight darkness, thumping among the breakers; and for a time they thought the whole ship's company must perish right there in their destined port; but by cutting away the masts they finally succeeded in saving the hull, cargo, and passengers.

The captain was subsequently known in San Francisco as Judge Shepherd. He brought a few very mean men to California; but also some as noble and good, perhaps, as ever landed in that port; such men, for example, as Calvin Lathrop, who for seven years was favorably known in California in the various relations of minister of the Gospel, Bible-class leader, gold digger, and clerk, and who filled so efficiently and satisfactorily for years the office of publishing agent of the *California Christian Advocate.* He has returned to his family in New-York, but is a thorough Californian still, and pants for the pure breezes of the Pacific. I wish it suited his family to go; he is needed in California.

It was several weeks after my arrival in San Francisco before I heard anything of my fellow-missionary, Rev. Isaac Owen, who had started with his family "across the plains" about the time I sailed from Baltimore. I felt great solicitude for his welfare, having heard much of the hazards of the overland route to California. After a few weeks, however, my mind was relieved by the news of his safe arrival in Sacramento City. Nearly four months had now elapsed, and yet we had not seen each other, neither having had time to visit the other. Friday, the fourth of January, 1850, found me making preparations to go to Sacramento City to see my colleague. First, I had to provide for my pulpit the Sabbath I should be absent, and I found a supply in James M'Gowan and M. E. Willing, local preachers, lately arrived in the ship Arkansas. Second, I had to lay in a good supply of firewood to keep my wife and babies warm during my absence.

Wood in the market was forty dollars per cord, and very poor stuff at that. I couldn't afford to burn wood at those rates.

The sand hills back of where I lived had been thickly covered with evergreen scrub oaks, but they had all been cut off, clean as a newly-mown meadow. I, however, took my ax and went to work on a stump, and soon found, to my agreeable surprise, that more than half the tree was under ground; that the great roots spread out horizontally just under the surface; so I had a good supply of wood at the simple cost of cutting, and loading it on my wheel-barrow and rolling it home. I had made a rare discovery, but, like the darkey who first struck the rich gold lead in "Negro hill," I soon had plenty of men to share my fortune.

The said colored man, I am told, went into the mines to dig some gold for himself, and thinking the "diggins" all free for everybody, he struck into the first good-looking place he came to. Presently along came a rough-looking miner, who said, angrily, "What are you doing there in my claim, you black rascal?"

"O massa, I didn't know dis are your claim!"

He then went off a little way, and saw a hole in which he thought he might find gold, so he jumped into it and went to work; but immediately a man came running at him in a rage, and shouted:

"Get out o' my hole, you cursed nigger, or I'll knock your head off!"

"Lor'sa, massa, me didn't know dis are your hole! Good Lor'sa, massa, where must I go?"

"Go up on the top of that hill, and dig," replied the miner, not dreaming that there was gold there; for as yet the value of hill diggings had not been found out.

But the poor old colored man went on the hill, and "sunk a shaft," (just like digging a well,) and wrought there several months, when it was discovered that he had struck a "rich lead," and was taking out the "big lumps." He then soon had plenty of company to share in his rich discoveries. The hill was afterward known as "Negro hill," and has yielded hundreds of thousands of dollars.

By Friday night I had my arrangements all made for an early start next morning for Sacramento City.

CHAPTER IV.

MISSIONARY LIFE — CONTINUED.

On Saturday, January 5, 1850, at 7 o'clock A. M., I embarked on the steamer Senator for Sacramento City, a distance of one hundred and twenty-five miles. As we ascended the Sacramento River we saw a large band of elk. They ran along the bank of the river in our direction several hundred yards, seeming as desirous to look at us as we were to look at them. On the sharp crack of a rifle in the hands of one of our passengers they changed their course, and gave us a wider berth, and soon disappeared in their own wild woods. A buck elk, with a head of full-grown horns, leaping over the hills, is a majestic looking animal.

Arriving in Sacramento City at 7 o'clock P. M., I was conducted by a stranger through one vast mud-hole of nearly half a mile to the house of Dr. Grove W. Deal. I had known the doctor well in Baltimore, and loved him much; saw him about a year before embark for California in the schooner Sovereign, via Panama, and often, during a tedious voyage round Cape Horn, comforted myself with

SACRAMENTO CITY.

the anticipated joy of meeting him on my arrival in San Francisco. This, however, was the first sight I had got of him in California. The doctor, I had learned, had done a great deal of faithful preaching "under the oak" in Sacramento City; and prior to Brother Owen's arrival, exercised a shepherd's care over the "few sheep in the wilderness." He had also succeeded well in his practice as a physician, besides some good trading "strikes," so that I did not find him in a tent, nearly up to his knees in mud, like most of his neighbors, but occupying one of the best houses in the city. It was a small, two-story frame-house, rough boards outside, and canvas lining inside. The first floor was occupied as a store, owned by the doctor, William Prettyman, another old Baltimore friend, and a young man whose name I have forgotten. They had in the store an assortment of clothing, dry goods and groceries, hardware, miners' tools and drugs, books and stationery, and such other varieties as the denizens of a new country were likely to need. The upper story was used as a reception-room, parlor, doctor's office, dormitory, etc. In the rear of the store was a shed made of rough slabs; the floor was of matting, to hide the mud, and to keep the passengers above ground; this was the wash-room, storage-room, kitchen, dining-room, etc.

There I received a hearty welcome, and found a noble-hearted, jovial set of fellows, and there we talked, and ate, and slept, and thanked the Lord, and talked again. The conversation now turning on the days of other years, and the loved ones on the other side of the continent, and now on the wonderful country into which our lot had fallen, and then the stirring incidents of the voyage, and the ever-exciting "news of the day." On Sabbath I accompanied the doctor to our "Baltimore California chapel," and was there introduced to Brothers Owen and Corwin.

I will not attempt to give a history of Brother Owen. Dr. Thurston, who, for the last five years, has been gathering materials in California for a book, asked Brother Owen to give him a sketch of his life for his book. After looking over a list of autobiographic notices in the doctor's book, by different ministers, and observing that special reference was made to the cities in which they had lived, and the colleges in which they had graduated, he penned something like the following: "Isaac Owen was born in Vermont, raised in Coon range on White River, in the wilderness of Indiana; costumed in buckskin, fed on pounded cake; educated in a log school-house. First book, Webster's spelling-book; first lesson in two syllables, commencing with 'Baker.' Converted in the woods, licensed to preach on a log; first circuit, then called Otter Creek Mission, embraced a part of five counties. Last heard of, a missionary in California, and on a review of his life has no apologies to offer for having been born." Brother Owen is a thick-set, rotund man, about five feet ten inches high, eyes and hair black, face round, with an easy, pleasant smile on his countenance. He is a good preacher, voice clear and strong, his preaching earnest and practical, characterized by clear Scripture expositions and familiar illustrations. Besides a thorough, practical education in real life, he has made himself quite familiar with his Greek Testament.

He is a man of indomitable energy and perseverance. I once heard Bishop Morris say of him that "Owen never gives up; he always does what he undertakes; if he can't do it one way he will another." He is apt in expedient in every emergency. He says he never was lost but once, and that was when a little boy. He was away in the wilderness alone; night was settling down upon him; the woods were full of wolves, wild cats, and panthers; and he knew not which way to go. After a little cogitation an expedient struck him. He cut a rod, caught his dog, and gave him a severe flogging, then letting the dog go, he instinctively cut for home as fast as he could run, and young Owen after him at the top of his speed. He thus got his bearings, and safely reached home a little after dark.

He says he never was in "straitened circumstances" but once. He had been out on a hunt, and got his buckskin trowsers very wet; coming home very wet and cold, he got into the fireplace of one of the old-fashioned wide chimneys, and stood by a blazing fire to warm himself. Being very much chilled, he could not feel the heat at once, till he felt something drawing very tightly about his legs; and now the heat seemed to be taking the skin off him; lo, his trowsers were drawn up into crisp, searing and singeing him; but though he jumped round, and cried for help, he could not pull them off. Said he: "I found myself that time in decidedly straitened circumstances."

Brother Owen is one of the greatest beggars in the world. He was for five years the agent of the Indiana Asbury University; so that besides natural talent for it, he is thoroughly skilled in the business. When he thinks a certain portion of a man's money ought to be appropriated to a special church enterprise in which he is engaged, (and he always has one such on hand,) and gets after him, that man had just as well, like old Dan Boone's coon, give up at once.

Rev. James Corwin had been a member of the same conference (Indiana) with Brother Owen, and located to accompany him to California, first, to help him with his family across the plains, and, secondly, to enter into the itinerant work with him on the Pacific.

He is a preacher of medium talent, faithful as a pastor, acceptable to the people, and very useful, not only in getting sinners converted, but in building churches and parsonages. He has no family of his own, but builds for those who have. After helping Brother Owen to build a parsonage for his family in Sacramento City, he took an appointment, and has been in the regular work ever since.

On the Sabbath morning above referred to, at Brother Owen's request, I preached to a full house, from, "God commendeth his love toward us, in that, while we were yet sinners, Christ died for us." Brother Owen preached at three P.M., and I again in the evening.

The next day the doctor and I dined with Brother Owen's family, and a sumptuous dinner it was, too; roast pork, sweet potatoes, and a variety of good things, hardly to be expected in California at that day. Brother Owen and wife had hardly recovered from the wear and tear of their long journey across the plains. They had a hard time in getting to California, and a sad reverse after their arrival.

Though I could hear nothing of them for several weeks after my arrival, they had reached the northern part of the territory about the same time that I reached San Francisco; and he preached near where the town of Grass Valley is now located, on the same Sabbath in which I commenced operations in the

Bay city. Thence he came on by land as far as Benicia, *en route* to San Francisco, and there learned that he had been appointed by the superintendent to Sacramento City, nearly one hundred miles back in the direction he had come. They were all nearly worn out, and to haul their effects back that distance, with a broken-down ox-team, was too much to think of enduring, so they engaged a sail-vessel to take their things to Sacramento City, and thus relieve their broken-down animals. The vessel was capsized, and they lost nearly everything they had in the world, all the supplies they had hauled across the continent.

When they got to Sacramento City, therefore, they were destitute of everything but the rough traveling clothes in which they appeared. They lived for a short time in a small tent, but Brother O. soon got able to move around among the people, and went to work with his usual zeal.

In a short time the chapel was up and ready for use, and he was at the time of my visit in a new parsonage, that cost about five thousand dollars. The society was in prosperous condition, and they had pledged themselves to give their minister a salary of four thousand dollars; one thousand dollars of which, however, Brother Owen appropriated toward the payment for the parsonage.

We walked and talked together for several days,

and laid the basis of an intimate and solid mutual friendship, which has remained unbroken to the present time, and will, I have no doubt, last forever We also matured plans for future operations. A book depository was to be established, and the country supplied with a pure religious literature; academies and a university were to be founded for the education of the rising generation; but at present we had to explore, and organize societies, so far as possible, without neglecting the charges to which we had been appointed. We agreed that I should, in addition to my work in San Francisco, travel south to San Josè and Santa Cruz, and organize societies; and that he should do what he could north of San Francisco, and thus prepare the way for other missionaries. We spent a part of Wednesday, the ninth of January, in Dr. Deal's upper room; and in the afternoon, when we came down to return to the parsonage, lo! a river came rolling down the street, meeting us. Half the city was already submerged, and the swelling flood hasted to bury the remainder. A wagon happened to pass near us at that moment, and Brother Owen paid the driver two dollars to take him a couple of blocks, whence he got a boatman to ferry him home. I took refuge in the doctor's house till after tea; but as the tide was still rising, and as I preferred to go to sea in a boat rather than a house, I commended my Baltimore friends to the mercy of the floods, and waded as best I could to the steamer Senator, and put up for the night.

The scene next morning is briefly described in my journal as follows:

"*Thursday, January* 10, 1850.—This morning I went up on the foretop of a store-ship anchored near our steamer, to take a survey of an entire city under water. I could not discover a single speck of land in sight, except a little spot of a few feet on the levee near our boat. The boatmen were navigating the streets in whale boats in every direction."

That day I returned to San Francisco, accompanied by Brother Corwin, who was on his way to Stockton, where he organized a society, and built a church and parsonage, partly by subscription and in part by his own hands; he, like the great Prophet of Nazareth, being a carpenter as well as a preacher.

We paid for our meals aboard the Senator two dollars each; the price of a state-room for one night was ten dollars; the fare alone from San Francisco to Sacramento City was thirty dollars. Charles Minturn, the agent in San Francisco, gave me a free passage up; and through the mediation of Captain Gelson I obtained a similar favor in Sacramento City, by which on that single trip I saved sixty dollars. Brother Corwin, however, not being considered exactly in the regular succession, had to pay his fare.

Captain Gelson, as one of the owners of the steamer M'Kim, that plied between the two cities named, offered a free passage to all *regular* ministers—those sent out as missionaries, or those having pastoral charges. I believe in that way the precedent was established; at any rate it became a custom with the owners and agents of steamboats running on the Sacramento and San Joaquin Rivers to give to all regular ministers a free ticket; and when the "California Steamboat Navigation Company" was organized, they adopted that as an item in one of their by-laws. They subsequently thought that the privilege was abused; that preachers multiplied too fast for the wants of the country; in other words, that many who were not pastors, and possibly not preachers at all, took advantage of it.

It was said, for example, that a man took passage on a Sacramento boat for himself and a lot of mules. When the captain demanded his fare he replied, "O, I'm a preacher, sir." "Indeed!" said the captain, and, pointing to the mules, inquired, "and are these preachers, too?" The fellow had to "walk up to the captain's office and settle." In consequence of these abuses the company passed a resolution making it necessary for all ministers wishing to travel on their boats to apply to the president of the company, who would, on the evidence that they were ministers, give them a free ticket.

Upon the whole, the liberality of California steamboat companies toward ministers of the Gospel stands unrivaled in the history of steamboat navigation, and has saved to the preachers (all of them poor enough in regard to means) an expense in traveling amounting to an aggregate of thousands of dollars. Stage proprietors in California have also shown a commendable liberality in the same way.

The Sacramento flood prevailed for days, bearing on its heaving bosom the tents and small buildings of the city, and a large proportion of their stock, consisting principally of horses, mules, cows, and oxen, which had been brought over the plains by hundreds. There was but little opportunity of saving the stock, because the valley, for the width of several miles, and in length for more than a hundred miles, was an unbroken sea of waters. The dwellers of the inundated city took refuge in the second stories of the few houses that remained, and in boats, and in the vessels that lay at anchor in the river. Our Baltimore chapel was carried from its foundations into the street, but not seriously injured. Brother Owen and family, after a few days' imprisonment in the upper story of their parsonage, determined to move to San José Valley, a distance of one hundred and seventy-five miles, and seek a place of residence on dry land. Sacramento City was inundated two or three times, which led to the construction of a strong levee around it, and it is hence frequently called the "Levee City." Much sickness prevailed there in early days, and thousands of sturdy adventurers sleep their last sleep on her low grounds; but it has become a very beautiful and healthful city, with a population, within eight years, of between twenty and thirty thousand.

On the 17th of January Brother Owen and family arrived in San Francisco, on their way to San José Valley. To give themselves some time for recuperation and preparations for their new home in San José, they made a temporary settlement in "Asa White's house with the blue cover," which, naturally enough, in view of the migratory character of its owners, was vacant at that time.

Having Brother Owen in the city to fill my pulpit, I embraced the opportunity to fulfill a promise to visit San José and Santa Cruz. Mrs. Taylor being out of health, and having the care of her babes and household duties, I thought it necessary to get some one to assist her during my absence. A Sister Merchant, an old maiden lady, had arrived a few weeks before, having made the voyage of Cape Horn, passing the dreary hours of the trip in composing *poetry*. She was sincerely pious, no doubt, and uttered many shrewd and sensible sayings; and yet it was evident that somewhere in her mental constitution there was a screw loose; still she was regarded as a valuable helper in the family; she said she could do everything in that line that could be desired. So I thought it would be a fine arrangement to have Sister Merchant as company for Mrs. Taylor, and to relieve her of the housework till I should return. The idea of a regular servant in a preacher's family, when servants got larger salaries than preachers, was out of the question. The preachers and their wives had to serve each other, and both together serve the children and the people. I know a California presiding elder who used to roll up his sleeves, and spend a day over the wash-tub as regularly as he went to quarterly meeting. I have turned out many a washing of clothes, and baked many a batch of bread, and think I understand the details of kitchen-work better than I do book-making. There were, however, preachers in California who would not hazard their ministerial dignity in the kitchen, or over the wash-tub, but were contented to let their wives struggle through all such drudgery alone, at whatever hazard.

Mrs. Taylor tells the following in regard to one of this class:

"I said to a missionary on arriving, whose delicate wife seemed ill-fitted for the labor and toil of pioneer life, 'You will have to help do the washing.' 'Not I,' replied the brother; and to my certain knowledge he never did. How appropriate! how considerate! a delicate female toiling at the tub over her dear lord's linen, while he sits complacently reading or puffing his havana, now and then yawning from pure laziness, and inquiring, 'Dear, when will dinner be ready?' as if there were a cook in the kitchen, or a nurse minding the infant, whose cries were heart-rending to the sympathizing mother. A man should not wonder if his gentle, sweet Mary, by such multiplied cares, unassisted, in the course of time seem unlike the youthful,. happy girl he took from the old folks at home."

Sister Merchant was very much pleased with the idea of living in the preacher's family—always loved the preachers and their wives. She had been sick, but had fully recovered, and was ready "to take all the work off Mrs. Taylor, and nurse the baby too." I thought myself highly favored in getting my pulpit and my family so well provided for during my contemplated absence of two weeks, and myself well provided with a traveling companion in the person of Brother J. Bennett, an exhorter in our Church, who was then on his way from the mines in Coloma to his family in Santa Cruz. On Saturday, January 19th, at half past nine A. M., we took passage aboard a little steamer for San José; distance, fifty miles, forty-two by water and eight by land; fare, twenty-five dollars each on the steamer, and five dollars per stage for the land travel to the town.

We reached the *embarcado* at five P. M., and concluded to save our stage fare by working our own passage thence to the town. After three hours hard wading through mud and water to our knees, we reached Widow White's house, within half a mile of town, and there obtained supper and lodging. Next day, at eleven A. M., I preached in the house of old Mr. Young, from "Fear not, for they that be with us are more than they that be with them." We had a refreshing class-meeting after preaching, consisting of more than "twelve persons."

Several American families, principally from Kentucky and Missouri, had settled there as early as 1846, and others later; in all now numbering about thirty, among whom were several Methodist families, namely: William and Thomas Campbell, and families, Captain Joseph Aram, a member of the convention that framed the constitution of the state, and family. Old Mr. Young was not then a Methodist, but his wife was, and their house was the preaching-place and the preacher's home. Charles Campbell, a local preacher, had been preaching there regularly for several months. Several Cumberland Presbyterian families also united with us, until such time as it might be practicable for them to organize for themselves; of whom were J. M. Jones and Asa Finley, with their excellent wives, and others.

That night I preached at Mr. Young's again, and many rejoiced with tears that the long desired day had come, when they should hear the voice of a regular minister, and be gathered into a fold, and receive the ordinances of the Lord's house. The next day Brother Bennet and I tried to get a horse to carry us over the creeks and rivers, and assist us on our way to Santa Cruz; distance, thirty miles by mule trail across the rugged coast-range of mountains. We might have walked, but did not like to wade the streams; and besides, Brother Bennet had a heavy "miner's pack," which we had carried alternately the Saturday night before until we thought it decidedly cheaper to employ the aid of a little horse-power. We found that the cheapest rate at which we could hire a horse was eight dollars per day, and as I did not expect to return for ten days, a very short calculation convinced us that "that would not pay."

Finally we succeeded in buying, for eighty dollars, a young red horse, very poor, hair all turned the wrong way, his mane pulled out by the roots, and his head nearly off. He had been tied to a mule, which ran away with him, and dragged him half a mile by the neck; and really, if he had not been a better horse than his appearance indicated, it would have killed him. Much has been said about the fine, fat horses of the itinerancy, and verily if the legions of Methodist cavalry connected with the nine thousand three hundred and forty traveling preachers of the United States were marshaled in one grand cavalcade, we should hardly know which most to admire, the noble horses or their heroic, self-sacrificing riders.

However illustrious the line of itinerant horses in California may become, let it be remembered that the specimen we have exhibited is the head of the succession, the *bona fide* St. Peter of the whole fraternity; being the first member of that tribe ever admitted into the itinerancy in that territory, excepting, of course, the mule Brother Roberts used on one of his visits from Oregon, and afterward sold to Brother Owen on sight, unseen, but has never been seen since by any of the parties claiming. So as it is not best to keep the Church in doubt as to the true head, which would lead to endless and useless discussion, it is better to decide the question at once in favor of the red horse.

There were at the time of our purchase plenty of good horses out on the plains, but not available in time for our purposes; so we did the best we could. In the afternoon we rigged up our young charger to go on our journey a few miles, and lodge at the house of William Campbell. When we got to

Pueblo Creek, which was greatly swollen by the late heavy rains, we both mounted our new horse, but by the time he got us fairly into the stream, he fell down, and gave us both an immersion, and I thought would have drowned, if we had not helped him up. We then led him by the rein, and waded out, and proceeded on our way, rejoicing "that it was as well with us as it was."

Arriving at Brother Campbell's at nightfall, we immediately sent out an appointment for preaching that night, and got in all the neighborhood, consisting of three families and six travelers, and had a good meeting.

After preaching we went and spent the night with Asa Finley and family. They treated us with great kindness, and gave us an early breakfast of chickens and eggs, reputed to be a favorite dish with the preachers; the first and only place where I received such fare in California for nearly two years. The mountain scenery of that day's travel was beautiful, and grand beyond description. Now a grove of redwood trees of immense size, and now a vast field of wild oats, cut in every direction with the trails of deer and grizzly bears.

Crossing the foot-hills we passed a large herd of sheep, guarded by a shepherd's dog, who alone had the care of the flock. He kept between us and his sheep, and gave us to understand, by his growling, that we must keep a respectful distance, and not meddle with him or his charge.

Those dogs are very common in California, and guard the sheep committed to their care with ceaseless vigilance day and night. But for them the coyotes, which are very numerous, would make dreadful havoc among the sheep. I heard of a California dog that took special care of the weak lambs of his flock, and was frequently seen to pick up the lagging lamb, and carry it in his mouth to its mother. Such illustrious examples in the canine tribe excite feelings of profound contempt against those lazy dogs that do nothing but eat, and sleep, and snap at the children.

Ascending to the mountain summit, the view was enchanting. Looking eastward we saw the splendid valley of San José, adorned in its beautiful new dress of green, spotted over with large bands of cattle, horses, mules, and sheep. Looking westward, over mountain peaks, foot-hills, and valleys, a distance of twelve or fifteen miles, there lay the great Pacific, spread out in silent grandeur as far as our ken could scan the horizon, and six thousand miles beyond. Night overtook us in the mountains; and, having no moonlight, we had no small difficulty in finding our way out.

At Santa Cruz I found a class of about twenty members, among whom were four local preachers. One of the preachers was a young man of considerable talent, and was employed at a salary of two thousand dollars a year to teach the village school; and, at the request of the society, had taken the relation of temporary pastor and preacher until they could be supplied by a regular missionary. The society got along very prosperously till a short time before my visit, when a dispute arose between two of the most prominent members about a town lot. Party strife was now at the flood, and the little heritage of the Lord, it was feared, was about to be swept away. The Sunday before an altercation arose in the class-meeting, in which a number of members left the house, saying they did not wish to be considered members any longer. The elected preacher in charge tendered his resignation, the meeting was broken up in confusion, and many pious souls went home weeping, and "thought that all was lost, and they never should again have any more good meetings." The arrival of a missionary just at that juncture was regarded as opportunely providential. We went to work immediately, as per Discipline, and had the case arbitrated, and although the breach was not healed at once, the society was relieved and reunited, and the way prepared for the preaching of the Gospel.

On Saturday, at eleven A. M., I preached in the house of Elihu Anthony from, "Therefore, leaving the principles of the doctrine of Christ, let us go on unto perfection." Preached again at night. Sunday, at half past nine A. M., we held a love-feast, and a joyful feast it was. Preached at eleven A. M. in the school-house, on the Divinity of Christ, to a crowded house. Several Spanish families were present, and seemed to be greatly interested. After sermon I administered the sacraments of baptism and of the Lord's Supper. About twenty persons partook of the emblems of "the broken body and shed blood" of their blessed Lord for the first time in California, and a majority of them had been in the country ever since 1847. They had longed for such a privilege in their new home, and now their tears, and sobs, and shouts told of the gladness of their hearts.

After preaching that night, two of Brother Bennet's daughters presented themselves as seekers of religion, the first female penitents I had seen in California. I made a plan of preaching appointments for the local preachers, and left the work in their hands till I should return in the spring. I was much pleased with my visit. Santa Cruz is a delightful place, situated on the north side of Monterey Bay, enjoying a pleasant sea-breeze, in the midst of one of the most fertile spots in the country. The American portion of the population at that time was composed principally of families who had settled there before the gold discovery, and had their children growing up around them, and hence the place was more home-like than any other place I had seen in the territory. They had also the best school, and largest Sunday school, in the country. There were the Anthony, Case, Bennet, and Hecox families, and others that I took real pleasure in visiting.

On Tuesday, the 29th of January, I retraced my steps alone over the mountains to San José Valley. It rained on me the whole day, and for several hours in the morning the fog was so dense that I was in great doubt as to what direction I was steering. The narrow mountain path was in many places very steep, slippery, and dangerous. In one such place my little horse fell down, and finding that he was on the eve of taking a roll down the mountain, I sprang off on the upper side, and let him have his roll to himself. Such a slide would probably have killed a common horse, but the little fellow was very tough, and like some unpromising young preachers I have seen, there was a great deal of "out-come" in him, for I learned he afterward made a fine horse.

I met two Spaniards on the mountain, who asked me for matches, and wanted me to stop and talk, but I did not like the looks of the fellows much, and made no tarrying. By the time I got through the mountains night overtook me, and that part of the valley being a vast sea of water and mud, I lost my way. In trying to find Brother Finley's place, I came to an Indian hut, and had a great fight with half a dozen dogs. I waked up the Indians, but they could not understand my language, nor I theirs. Finally, at a late hour, I reached the "Mission of Santa Clara," now a flourishing town, and the seat of our university. I put up at an old adobe house, bearing the name of Reynolds' Hotel, and was conducted to the bar-room, where a jolly set of gamblers were engaged in card-playing. After getting myself warmed, and refreshed by a pretty good supper, the gamblers having finished their games for the night, I engaged them in conversation about California life, and sobered them down a little by a description of the condition of sick adventurers in the San Francisco hospitals. None of them knew me, but they treated me with respect, as most Californians will always treat any man who behaves himself, and attends to his own business. Finally one said:

"Well, boys, let's go to bed."

"Agreed," responded another.

Said I: "Gentlemen, if you've no objections, I propose that we have a word of prayer together before we retire."

They looked at each other and at me a moment, in evident surprise, when the bar-keeper, who was standing behind his bar, waiting an opportunity to sell to each fellow a retiring "nip" for twenty-five cents per head, said:

"I suppose, sir, there's no objection."

"Thank you, sir," said I, and added: "And now let us all kneel down, as we used to do with the old folks at home, and ask the Lord for his blessing."

I believe that every gambler of them kneeled down, as humbly as children, and I had a blessed season in praying for them, and for their mothers and sisters, whom they might or might not ever again see on mortal shores; but that the wandering adventurers in California, with their mothers and sisters at home, might all give their hearts to God, believe in Jesus, and be prepared for a happy greeting on the other shore, and a home in heaven.

They took no more *nips* that night, but slipped off to bed, mute as mice. I afterward met one of them in San José, and he took off his hat by the time he got within a rod of me. I said nothing to them on the subject of gambling. The next day I exchanged my little red horse for one that could carry me through the mud without falling down, at the hazard of his own neck and mine, and gave thirty dollars to boot. The next night I preached again at Mr. Young's in San José, had a good audience and profitable meeting.

On Thursday morning I started for San Francisco, distance fifty miles, through mud and water, a great part of the way, up to my horse's knees. I passed Whisman's before noon, the only public house on the road, or private one either, except two or three

"Spanish ranchos." I knew not where I was to spend the night, but determined to go as far as I could, and to stop wherever my horse gave out. Never having traveled that route, I went several miles out of my way; but met a Spaniard who kindly put me on my course.

About nine o'clock at night I reached San Franciskito Creek, which was booming and overspreading its banks. It made such a roaring and crashing that I tried in vain to get my horse into it, and the darkness was so dense that I could not tell where I was to land if he had gone in. Turning back I saw a light not far distant, and, approaching, found it to be a hunter's camp, occupied by three men, two of whom were very drunk. They granted me permission to lodge with them, that is, to warm by their fire, and sleep on the ground in a blanket they loaned me.

I staked my horse out to grass; for though the valley was flooded, it was covered with new grass, about eight inches high, and returning to the fire, the drunker man of the two met me, and said, "I want to have a word with you," and, staggering round behind the tent, he took my arm, and said, "Stranger, you mustn't mind anything that man there may say to you. He's a clever feller, but he's pretty drunk to-night. Stranger, you mustn't mind him."

After I seated myself by the fire the three men told their experience. The details were too horrible to be repeated. When they got through they wanted me to tell mine: so I gave them a little of my experience.

As I proceeded they stared at me, and finally one of them said, "You're a preacher, ain't you?"

"Yes," I replied; "I pass for one."

"O, good Lord, didn't ye catch us?" said they, with sundry apologies for their vulgar talk in the presence of a preacher. "We didn't dream that there was a preacher in the country."

After that they gave me extra attention, and I left them, after an early breakfast, feeling that I owed them a debt of gratitude, and homeward I went, expecting to find Mrs. Taylor quite recruited in health by the opportune aid of good Sister Merchant.

CHAPTER V.

MISSIONARY LIFE — CONTINUED.

On my return from Santa Cruz I learned that Sister Merchant, instead of being servant in the family, had assumed to be mistress, and had all hands, with a neighboring family added, to wait on her. The day after I left, by some means, *several more screws* got loose about her; indeed, she became crazy, and refused to do anything; said that "the Lord's children are kings and priests," and that she "was one of them sure," and that it did not become kings and priests to be doing housework. She also refused to leave; said that "the house was the Lord's, and that she was the Lord's, and had a right to stay there as long as she pleased; was astonished that Mrs. Taylor should have the audacity to speak to her about leaving the house of her heavenly Father; she knew Brother Taylor wouldn't do such a thing; that Brother Taylor was more sanctified than Sister Taylor, and that he would settle the question of right between them as soon as he got home, that he would."

She took possession of an upper room, which had

just been rented for fifty dollars per month, and refused to give it up to the person who had rented it, or to anybody else, and there remained day and night, demanding her meals regularly, and all other needful attention, and kept Mrs. Taylor and the children awake a good share of every night with her songs and prayers. Having no home nor friends, Mrs. Taylor would not have her turned out of doors, but patiently did her bidding. It was some time after my return before we could get her comfortable quarters elsewhere. In the mean time she righted up, so as to look out for herself. So much for our first experience with servants in California.

At that time we had no asylum for the insane in California, and yet such was the constant overstretching of mind and muscle, that a great many persons became deranged, and their condition was indeed deplorable. Some such were sent to the hospitals, some to the "Prison Brig," and some were confined in private outhouses, with about as much care as a wild animal would command. I remember one in the hospital who thought he was in prison and was suffering, and verbally detailing all the horrors of false imprisonment, dragged away from his family, and imprisoned for life, without ever letting him know with what offense he was charged. He wept and bewailed his desolate condition, nobody to plead his cause, and no hope of ever seeing his wife and children again."

When I would assure him that he was not in prison, but being unwell he was placed in that house, which the city had kindly provided for sick strangers, for medical treatment, and that he would soon be well, and could then go and see his family, "O, is that it! O, I'm so glad! I'm so glad!" he would rejoice a minute, and then slide back into his hopeless prison.

Another I used to see in the hospital, said he was Daniel Webster's private secretary. He was always cheerful, and polite as a French dancing-master. He was constantly receiving company. "Good morning, Commodore Perry. I'm very happy to see you so unexpectedly. Walk in, walk in, commodore. Give me your cap, and be seated. I'll call Mr. Webster. I know he'll be delighted to see you. He was speaking of you only this morning at the breakfast table. I was just reading, commodore, as you came to the door, one of your dispatches from the seat of war. That was a dreadful fight you had with the Philistines! The American navy never had such a contest before, and never before achieved so glorious a victory! All glory to the American navy! all honor to Commodore Perry! Let the stars and stripes float forever! I say."

Those two poor fellows were both harmless, and

occupied places in large wards filled with sick men.

But I used to see a man who was considered dangerous. He was tightly laced in a strait-jacket, and bound down to the ground floor of a basement room in the hospital, dark, damp, cold, and cheerless as *Hades*.

Poor fellow, how I pitied him in my very soul!

A Captain B. was taken to a hospital near where I lived, and was confined in a stable. He complained of very bad treatment, and at all hours we could hear his ravings. He tore off his own clothes, and must have suffered from cold. Mrs. Arington living near, getting permission of the doctor to visit the captain, and give him his meals occasionally, took him in hand, and treated him kindly; he ceased his ravings, and spent much of his time in lauding the dear woman who became his friend when he had none. He subsequently recovered.

In January, 1852, a state Lunatic Asylum was commenced in the city of Stockton, which has since received annual appropriations by the State Legislature for improvements, and for the cure of the insane.

The appropriations for the year 1854 amounted to one hundred and fifty-three thousand dollars. Eighty thousand of that amount was for the erection of a main building, which is thus described in the "Annual Reports of the Officers of the Insane Asylum of the State of California for the year 1854."

"The main building, just erected and finished, is a brick structure, seventy feet square, three stories high. The first story is fifteen feet in the clear, contains eight rooms and two halls, fourteen feet wide. The second story is twelve feet in the clear, contains sixteen rooms, with halls same as in the first story. The third story is eleven feet in the clear, contains eighteen rooms, with halls same as in the lower stories. There is a ventilator in every room, flues in all the rooms in the first story, and in all the principal rooms in the second and third stories. The height of the top of the spire from the ground is one hundred and nine feet, and height of top of pediment from the ground is sixty-one feet."

Table IV of said report, "shows the number of admissions, recoveries, discharges, deaths, and the number remaining in the hospital at the close of each year since the organization of the institution," up to the close of 1854:

	1852.	1853.	1854.	TOTAL.
Admissions	124	222	305	651
Recoveries	52	110	150	312
Deaths	10	12	21	43
Discharges	52	110	150	312
Remaining	62	103	134	299

A German gardener came to me, saying "that he had hired himself for a year, at a hundred dollars per month, to a Scotch gardener at the mission," and begged me, as a favor, to draw up an article of agreement for him, which, as a matter of accommodation, I did. Then, after getting it signed, he begged me, with the Scotchman's consent, to take care of it for him, so I locked it up in my private trunk. During my absence at Santa Cruz our little babe was taken very ill, and Mrs. Taylor, having no one to send for the doctor, went to the door, hoping to see some one pass whom she might send for a physician. Just as she got to the door she met the German gardener, accompanied by another, who demanded of her the said article of agreement. "It is with Mr. Taylor's papers," said she, "locked up in his trunk, and he has the key in his pocket, so you can't get it till he returns."

"We must have it," said they, "and if you don't give it up peaceably, we'll take it by force."

The sick babe was crying in the kitchen, the crazy woman was singing and shouting up stairs, and there were two savage-looking men contending against one sick woman. Mrs. Taylor replied: "I told you before that the paper was in that trunk, and I can't get it. If it is your mind to break open the trunk, you do it at your own risk," and with that she left them, and went to her babe. They then broke open my trunk by knocking the bottom out of it, and after rummaging through all my papers, letters, memoranda, etc., found their paper and left. So Mrs. Taylor had a fine opportunity for the development and exercise of her patience during my absence. The trunk breakers afterward learned that they had laid themselves liable to prosecution, and soon after I returned the gardener came to apologize, and offer to pay for the trunk. Colonel Nevins happened to be at my house when he came in. I told the fellow that I would not accept pay for the trunk; that to come in my absence, and frighten my sick family, and break open my trunk in that manner, was an offense not to be wiped out by paying the price of a trunk, and, continued I, here is Colonel Nevins, an old practitioner at the bar, I'll turn you over to him, and let him put you through as you deserve. The colonel heard the statement of the case and said to him: "My dear fellow, you have got yourself into a bad fix; you are guilty of a state prison offense; the evidence is all clear; a very plain case, and we'll have you in the chain-gang in less than thirty-six hours."

The old fellow dropped on his knees, and weeping like a whipped child, begged us to kill him; said he had "never been arrested for any offense in his life, had always tried to support a good character, and now in his old days to be put into the chain-gang was worse than death." So we had compassion on him, and after further admonition dismissed the case.

On going through the hospital, on my return, I was shocked to see what sad havoc death had made among the poor fellows with whom I had sympathized and prayed the day before I left the city. Having added a horse to the number of my family cares, I had occasion to take some new lessons in California prices. Bought a sack of barley, one hundred and fifty pounds, for fifteen dollars. Bought a hundred pounds of hay, miserable stuff too, for fifteen dollars, and carried it all home on my horse at one load. But having promised to preach occasionally at San José and Santa Cruz, and take the pastoral oversight of them, I found it cheaper to keep a horse, even at those rates, than to pay the enormous fare of public conveyances.

February 10th, 1850. Brother Owen and I, assisted by a few brethren, dug the foundation, and commenced the erection of a small book-room, adjoining our church on Powell-street. Carpenters' wages were so enormously high, twelve dollars per day, that we did most of the work with our own hands. Brother Owen, after his appointment to the missionary work in California, spent some time in collecting funds and books, and shipped for California about two thousand dollars' worth of books. They arrived per ship Arkansas, and on January 16th, 1850, I got them ashore, paying for lighterage five dollars per ton—fifteen dollars. They were discharged from the lighter on the sand beach, foot of California street, whence I had to heave the boxes fifty yards, to get them where they could be loaded on a dray. Paid forty dollars to have them hauled to my house on Jackson-street, where they remained unopened till February 16th, when we had them hauled to our new book-room. This was the nucleus of "The Book Concern of the Pacific;" and in the midst of our toil in establishing it, we contemplated with a good deal of satisfaction its future greatness and usefulness. As I was resident in the city, it devolved on me to attend to the books, which I did at the expense of a great deal of time and toil, in connection with the multiplied duties of the pastorate. It was so expensive hauling, that I generally packed on my shoulder the boxes and packages we sent out to order from the book-room to the boat, more than half a mile; but I thought nothing of time and labor, if we could thereby establish a good book depository, and supply the coast with a sound religious literature; for next to the preaching of a pure Gospel, we considered that most important for the redemption of the country from error and sin.

While Brother Owen's family still occupied Father White's shanty in San Francisco, their little daughter, two years old, took croup, or something similar, and on February 13th died. It was a beautiful child, and having carried it over the plains, it had become an early partner in their toils and sufferings, and had endeared itself to the family to a greater degree, perhaps, than children ordinarily do at that age. To see the old missionary and his wife join hands, as when they stood at Hymen's altar, and bow together over their dying babe, and impress on its fading cheek the parting kiss, was indeed a scene too touching for adequate description. The good brother bowed his head, and received the shock like a man of God inured to trial; but Sister Owen, dear woman, had been so worn down by hardship and toil, and her nervous system was so shattered, that the lightning bolt seemed to strike through her soul. The shock to her was so heavy that she has never fully recovered from its effects. She is still a sensible, pious woman, but evidently a wreck, physically, of what she has been in her days of sunshine and hope. Brother Treat Clark made her little girl's coffin, and I, assisted by Brother Hatler, dug tho grave; and there, on the northwest corner of the Powell-street Church lot, we buried the little jewel of Jesus, the first member of our mission to leave us; a hostage taken by the Master to bind that wayworn family more firmly to the land of their adoption, and to commit them more fully to the work of its redemption from sin and error.

Brother Owen built a small one-story house, half a mile east of the town of San José, into which he moved his family; and leaving them in care of his father-in-law, he on the 2nd of March returned alone to his charge in Sacramento City. The waters having assuaged, he had his church brought back to her moorings, and fulfilled the duties of his charge, in the absence of his family, till the close of that conference year.

On the 2nd of March, 1850, while I was at work in the book-room, Brother Troubody and a good-looking stranger came in, and I was introduced for the first time to Rev. William Roberts, our superintendent. The great pleasure of meeting a fellow-laborer, experienced by those in distant fields, where such meetings are like angel visits, can hardly be conceived by any but the subjects of it. Brother Roberts put up with us, and occupied our prophet's room. We felt it a great privilege to enjoy his company, not only on account of the novelty of it, but especially because he is a Christian gentleman of high order—one of the Lord's noblemen. He preached in our chapel at eleven A. M. next day, from, "Whosoever shall confess me before men, him shall the Son of man also confess before the angels of God." It was a pointed, practical sermon, which was to me as manna to the hungry soul. He preached again at night an excellent sermon on the witness of the Spirit. That day, at three P. M., I preached, from a pile of lumber on Mission-street, the funeral sermon of William H.

Stevens, who had died the day before, leaving in his distant home, Winnebago County, Illinois, a wife and six children. Death in California in those days seemed clothed with extraordinary terrors, without any of the mitigating circumstances attending the death-scenes of old settled communities. No kind sister's hand to wipe the death-sweat from the brow; nor affectionate wife to impress on the pallid cheek the parting kiss, and whisper words of peace in the ear of the dying; no gathering of the children around the departing father to receive his last, solemn charge, catch his last smile and lingering look. A little boy, for example, was seen crying in the street of San Francisco early one rainy morning in the winter of 1849–50, and a man said:

"Little boy, what's the matter with you?"

"Daddy's dead, and I don't know what to do with him!"

The lad conducted the man into a small tent, and there lay his dead father all alone. It was said that he owned a farm in Missouri, and had plenty of friends at home; but lingered and died, unknown to any but his little boy.

The circumstances attending the protracted illness of Brother Stevens were most distressing; but he was triumphant over all by the grace of Jesus, and said when dying, "Tell my wife I die in peace, and go home to heaven. I expect to meet her and the children there." This death-scene is described in detail in my "Seven Years' Street Preaching in San Francisco," p. 363.

Brother Roberts spent nearly four weeks in California at that time, two Sabbaths in San Francisco, and the rest of his time in Stockton and Sacramento City. He sailed for Oregon on the 29th of March. On the same day I made my second visit to San José, accompanied by my family.

We were met on our arrival by our old friend, Dr. Grove W. Deal, who was a representative from Sacramento in the Territorial Legislature, then in session in San José. The doctor filled his seat in the Legislature during the week, and preached the Gospel to his fellow-law-makers on the Sabbath.

I shall not attempt to report the good which he may have accomplished there, except to say that a bill for the incorporation of Church property was presented, in which it was provided that the trustees should be elected by the society, and the doctor had it so amended as to recognize any board of trustees duly elected or *appointed* according to the rules or discipline of the Church they might represent.

I saw an example six years afterward, of the practical importance of that amendment. An effort was made in a lawsuit to ignore the legal existence of a Methodist board of trustees. The lawyer on the other side said:

"This is not a legal board of trustees, because they never were duly elected by the society."

"True," replied another, "they were not elected by the society, but they were duly appointed by the preacher in charge."

"Yes," answered the other, "but, according to the statute, they must be *elected by the society*."

He had not read the statute lately, if ever, and did not know that when it was being molded it had passed through the hands of a Methodist preacher. He was then requested to read the statute, and he [illegible] his disappointment, that it decided against [illegible] point on which he had hung all his hopes of success in the suit.

On Saturday the 30th, I accompanied Doctor Deal to the Assembly Hall, and witnessed the election of the first district judges in the territory. Next day I preached at Mr. Young's, and also in the Senate Chamber. After preaching in the morning we had a blessed class-meeting. A Frenchman with a Spanish wife were in class, and upon Brother C. Campbell's recommendation were admitted into society on probation. They soon afterward moved away, and I know not what became of them.

On Monday, April 1, I opened a subscription for the erection of a Methodist Episcopal Church in San José. That was election day there for county officers, and hence a day of great excitement in town, but more especially because of a celebrated horse-race, which came off that afternoon. An American by the name of Hedgepeth, and a native Californian by the name of Pico, ran against each other for a prize of ten thousand dollars on each side. Such a stake was in keeping with the times, and such a scene the highest intellectual entertainment that could engage the attention of the masses. Hedgepeth took the prize.

I was abroad among the people making interest for my new church enterprise, but would not turn my head to see the race, which to many was matter of as great surprise as my apparent want of interest in the shark catching on my voyage to California.

One Sunday, in the South Pacific, just after preaching, I was seated on deck reading the Bible, when lo, a cry, "A shark! a shark!" All hands ran abaft to see the great man-eater of the deep. Many said to me as they passed, "Come and see the shark; he's a rouser." Several baited hooks were thrown out, swallowed, and bitten off. At one time they hooked it, and drew it up to the taffrail, when the line broke, and down it dropped. Finally they harpooned it, and, in the midst of universal shouting and hurraing, it was drawn aboard. It was a huge monster.

Colonel Myers returning from the scene, said to me, as I sat still reading the word,

"Did you not see the shark?"

"No, sir," said I.

"Why, not?" said he, with great surprise.

"I was engaged," replied I, "in reading the word of the Lord, which to me is of more importance than shark killing, especially on the Sabbath;" and added: "Colonel, if I were engaged in conference with a king on important business, and should in the midst of his conversation, on the occurrence of some trivial excitement, catching a shark, for example, jump up and leave him abruptly, I would be treating him with great disrespect, would I not? I have just been reading a message from, and holding a conversation with the GREAT KING, and I think to stop short and run away to see a fish killed on this his holy day, would not be treating him with becoming courtesy."

"True," said he; "that's consistent; you're right."

So in the great horse-race excitement I was engaged in preparing to build a house for the Lord; and I did not wish to give countenance to such entertainments.

After spending a couple of days in San José soliciting for our new church, and getting on subscription about two thousand dollars, I returned to San Francisco. My visit to the hospital the day after my return is thus noted in my journal:

"*April* 5, 1850.—Visited hospital this P. M. Eight or ten persons have died during my brief absence. C. W. Bradley, from Louisiana, died to-day while I was there. Said he, when dying: 'I am ready; I resign all to Jesus. Tell my wife to meet me in heaven.'

"Poor M., one of the men I rescued from the other hospital, (see "Seven Years' Street Preaching in San Francisco," etc., p. 66,) died cursing and swearing in the bitterest despair.

"D. is an honest-looking pioneer, a man of good common sense and information; has been religiously educated, has a Methodist wife at home, but is sinking to the grave without salvation. He says: "It's so presumptuous, now that I'm dying, to offer myself to God; I cannot do it. It is impossible for me to receive pardon!'"

These are but specimens of a various multitude of cases. The day after the above was penned I was called to see Dr. G. He lay in a small shanty on a sand hill, near what is now the corner of Montgomery and Pine streets; and as his case will illustrate the condition of hundreds whom I have seen encounter death on those distant shores, I will give a brief description of it.

He was an intelligent man, had been favored with good literary and religious educational advantages, had a pious wife at home; but there he was, an isolated stranger among strangers, reduced to penury, far gone with chronic diarrhea, utterly dispirited, no hope in this life, and worse than all, no hope beyond the grave. Said he: "I have always known it was my duty to serve God, and have had a great many invitations to accept of mercy through Christ; but, though outwardly moral, I have lived a great sinner against God all my life, and now I'm caught! I'm caught at last! God is about to call me to judgment without mercy."

I urged him to seek God's favor, and trust in the merits of Jesus.

"Too late now," said he; "I have been so presumptuous and wicked there's no hope for me. I sometimes catch at something that inspires a little hope, but again lose my hold, and all is darkness. There appears to be a thick vail between God and my soul; a bar that I cannot get over. I feel that when I leave this world I shall have *no home and no employment!* I wish I never had been born! For what purpose have I had an existence? The world could have done without me; I've done no good in it! I might have been saved, but I refused; and now I must be the personification of everything that is despicable, and wretched, and mean forever!"

I talked, and sung, and prayed, and did everything I could to inspire a hope in the poor fellow's heart, in the light of which he might find his way to the cross of Jesus, but all without effect.

At another time when I called to see him, for I saw him frequently, he said:

"I have been trying since you were here to seek Jesus, but I cannot find him."

When I represented to him the mercy of God in Christ, he replied:

"God has given me commandments to keep, but I have broken them all my life. I often felt guilt and sorrow for my sins, but did the same things again, and now God has gone from me."

I then gave him the Saviour's illustration of importunity in seeking, and his encouraging command and promise: "Ask and ye shall receive; seek and ye shall find; knock, and it shall be opened unto you."

"I fain would ask," replied he; "but when I try I talk to vacancy, I find not the ear of God; I know not how to seek, and I cannot find the place to knock."

Alas! thought I, poor Esau; birthright gone, and no place for repentance. How my soul pitied him. I then said, "O my dear brother, you must not give yourself up to despair."

"It has given itself to me," said he; "it covers my soul with the pall of death, and overwhelms me in darkness without hope."

Soon after this interview, when death struck him, he begged most imploringly: "Help me up! O do help me up! Set me down on the floor."

He was helped out of bed by those present, and gasped and died before they could get him back. What madness and folly to postpone the great business of life, for the accomplishment of which the Lord does not give us too much time nor strength, to such an hour, when time and strength have fled.

Wednesday, April 10, found me on my way a second time to Santa Cruz, to organize a quarterly conference, and hold a meeting. Before starting that morning I sold a lot of Methodist books to a Brother Walker, to take to New South Wales; also sold my horse to W. O. Johnson for one hundred and fifty-two dollars, reserving two trips on him to Santa Cruz, thereby securing the end without the risk and expense of keeping him. Bought him to save expense; amount saved, one hundred and sixty dollars; sold him to save expense; cost in the country one hundred and ten dollars; brought in the city one hundred and fifty-two dollars. Johnson afterward told me he was a "lucky horse" for him; said after making ten thousand dollars in California, his livery stable was burned, and everything in it except "Charley." He had to begin the world again with nothing but that horse, but started the same business with him, and in two years regained all he had lost.

I did better with that horse than I did with the mule on which I traveled a couple of months in the mines. Bought the mule for ninety dollars, rode him about two hundred miles, and fell in with a "packer," who claimed him, and proved property; but in consideration of my having bought him before in good faith, he sold him to me for fifty dollars. When I returned from the mountains I put him in charge of a man who had a "ranch" on Sacramento River, to have him recruited, and took his receipt. When I sent to get the mule, the "ranch" was still there, but the man, mule, saddle, bridle, and all, "had gone to other diggins," and I have not heard of them since.

The following scrap from my journal notes an incident of that trip to Santa Cruz:

"*Friday, April* 12, 1850.—On my way to quarterly meeting in Santa Cruz; now seated at one P.M. under the shade of an ancient oak, which stands on the summit of the coast range of mountains between San José Valley and the Pacific Ocean, from which both are in view. I am in the midst of one of nature's grand pasture fields of wild oats and grass. While my horse is grazing, having taken my cold lunch alone, I have just had a precious season of prayer 'on the mount.' Jesus often went up into a mountain to pray. I have prayed on many a mountain on both the Eastern and Western slopes of the continent, and have always found the mount a good place for prayer. Its pure air, its grand impressive scenery, its altitude, bearing you away heavenward far above the din and bustle of the babbling world beneath.

"Jesus had a reason for going up into a mountain to pray. I now mount my horse and travel on; very warm; have to walk a great deal, because of the roughness and danger of the way. Half past four P. M., have just got through the mountain, and seated myself in the midst of one of nature's most beautiful flower-gardens to rest.

"The Lord has lavished more beauty on California than upon any spot I have ever seen. The perfect transparency of her atmosphere, the salubriousness of her climate, the sublimity of her mountains, the invigorating freshness of her ocean breezes, the beauty of her valleys, and the variety and extent of her native flower-gardens, carpeting hill and dale for miles together with all the colors of light, are quite without a parallel anywhere in 'Uncle Sam's' dominions, if not in the world.

"For a couple of miles back, as I came through a dense chaperel thicket, I have been on the track of a grizzly bear. His track, by measurement, was fourteen inches long and seven wide; he must have been a monster. I was on the look-out at every turn of the path to see him start up before me, and wondered whether or not he would clear the track. The path was cut so deeply by the winter torrents, and was in many places so narrow, that there was no chance to wheel and retreat. I, however, felt but little fear, for I regard old grizzly as one of my Father's domestics, and can't hurt me without his consent; still, if I saw him coming, and had room, I should be like the fellow I heard of a few days ago. He got rather close to an old grizzly in this very mountain, and bruin took after him as fast as he could run, and the fellow almost killed his mule getting out of the way; but he cleared the track, and saved his mule meat and his own as well."

Organized and held our quarterly conference on Saturday, April 13th, at four o'clock P. M. Renewed the preaching license of E. Anthony, A. A. Hecox, H. S. Loveland, and Enos Beaumont; and at that meeting licensed Alexander M'Lean to exhort. He afterward became a very useful young preacher in California, but feeling it his duty to take a course at the Biblical Institute in Concord, we very reluctantly gave him up, hoping that he would afterward go into the work in California. He took his course; I believe graduated, and is still a preacher, though not in the itinerant work. I am decidedly in favor of the thorough preparation of mind and heart for the work of the Christian ministry; but when a man is called of God to preach the Gospel, and in the order of Providence is as actively and efficiently committed to the work as was Brother M'Lean, I very much question whether it is his duty to leave the *regular* work to go to Concord, Jericho, or anywhere else. I have no doubt that Brother M'Lean is useful wherever he is, but I think he ought to be wholly devoted to the ministry. He is a very capable young man.

On my way to the meeting above referred to, I put up at a public house, where they made no charge except for my horse, and invited me to stay with them whenever I could; said they were "always glad to see the preachers." Returning, I spent a night at the same place, and took with me three travelers, who designed going elsewhere. My host talked very kindly to me, but charged us all alike, five dollars and fifty cents each for our night's lodging and breakfast. I could not account for the change of his conduct toward me, unless, 1st, his covetousness got the mastery of his "kind feelings for the preachers;" or, 2d, his wife, who seemed to be the personification of grasping cupidity, charged him to charge me.

He was like a *Christian* an old sailor tells about. "There is a clothing merchant up in Boston," said Jack, "who keeps that command in the Scriptures where it says, 'Thou shalt take the stranger in.' I was a stranger and he took me in bad on a pea-jacket I bought of him."

On my return to San Francisco, I learned that the first missionaries from the Methodist Episcopal

Church, South, Dr. Jesse Boring, and Brothers Pollock and Winn had arrived. Up to that time, Methodism in California had been as true to its native instincts—devotion of heart to God, and the union of a common brotherhood, through that favorite nursery of Christian sympathy, the class-meeting—as the needle to the pole; a unit; no North nor South ever mentioned. The only question they ever asked me on their arrival, anywhere from Maine to Florida was, "Are you a Methodist preacher?" "Yes, sir, I pass for one." "I thought so," was generally the reply, followed by another, "shake hands," and a hearty, mutual congratulation on the enjoyment of the blessings and privileges of our common Methodism on the Pacific coast. And I really thought by burying all local prejudices, and by uniting the cool, calculating heads of the North, and the warm hearts of the South in one body, and then have that body in vested with the characteristic energy of California life, and then have all sanctified to God, we would raise up on the Pacific coast the greatest people in the world. I must say, therefore, that I looked with fearful apprehension upon an effort to make "*twain*" of that which, I thought, for the honor and efficiency of our common Methodism in California, should be but ONE. I immediately went, however, and called on the newly arrived brethren of the Church, South.

My feelings and views in regard to them are expressed in my journal as follows:

"*Thursday, April* 18, 1850.—Learned on my return to-day, that the representation of the Southern Church had arrived, and in company with Dr. B. Miller, I called and spent an hour with them. They avow neutrality on the slavery question; say they do not believe that slavery ever will exist in California, but that the Church, South, as a Christian Church, claim the privilege of sending missionaries to China, California, or wherever they think they can do good. I take them to be Christian men, and true ministers of the Gospel, and as such I shall treat them till they convince me that I am mistaken. There is a great work for Christian men and ministers to do in California, and if the Lord has sent these men here to help do it, I pray that he may open their way for harmonious action with other Churches, and give them great success in saving souls; if the Lord has not sent them here, I hope he will send them back where they came from, and the sooner the better. I shall leave them in his hands, and not attempt to drive them away. I shall give them a welcome to my pulpit and to my heart, as men of God, while they act as such.

Brother Pollock was stationed in Sacramento City, and was cordially received by Brother Owen, who not only invited him to his pulpit, but gave him a list of the names of all his members who had come from the South. I did not feel like going quite so far as that. Many of my members were from the South, and I loved them. They had joined my Church voluntarily, without a word of persuasion, and I thought now, if they wish to leave and join the Church, South, they may report themselves and go as they came. One or two felt it their duty to go, and I did not blame them. The greater number thought it their duty to remain with us, and I thought they did right to do so.

But I am clearly of the opinion, that however sincere and holy the ministers of both parties, one organization of Methodism in California would accomplish at least twice the amount of good in the salvation of sinners, and the redemption of that fair land, than the *two* are accomplishing, or can accomplish. True, we have not spent much time and ammunition in fighting each other, and never expect to; but our relative position is such that there are hundreds, and probably thousands, who would have been warm friends of either branch had it been alone, who will commit themselves to neither, situated as we are. I will illustrate the truth of this view of the subject by a specimen case. J. D. Hoppe, a merchant in San José, member of the convention that framed the constitution of the state, a friend to Methodism, had been a Church member in Missouri, gave me a subscription of one hundred dollars for our church there, and verbally promised two hundred dollars more as we progressed in the work; but afterward, hearing of the arrival of the Southern representation, he said to me: "By the organization of two Methodist Churches in California you are going to have collision and strife, and I'll have nothing to do with either party of you. I'm sorry I promised to help you with your church. The hundred dollars I subscribed I'll pay," handing it to me at the same time; "but I'll subscribe no more, and pay no more to either party of you." I believe he kept his word to the day of his death. The poor fellow died in San Francisco about three years after, from burns received in the explosion of the steamer "Jenny Lind." I believe a legion of similar illustrations could be produced.

The chapel we built in San José during the summer of 1850 is still in use by a flourishing society and Sunday school: a good station, giving support to a preacher and family.

As a bit of personal experience in California, I will insert a birthday notice from my journal:

"*Thursday, May* 2, 1850. I am this day twenty-nine years of age. How astonishing to me that I am entering my thirtieth year. I feel like a boy. I have not at all, as yet, realized my aspirations for literary and spiritual attainment, nor my ideal of manhood,

If I may judge of the future by the past, I shall never learn much from books. Inestimable treasure lies locked up in my library, but I do not take time to count it out and use it; always intending to do so, but always attending to other duties, such as visiting the sick, looking after Book Depository, answering the ten thousand questions asked by strangers, just arriving, about California, etc., my time is cut up into so many fragments that it appears to be lost. I am spread over so much surface that I cannot concentrate what I consider effective force at any one point. O Lord, in whatever else I am disappointed, let me live in thee, and win souls to Christ! Twenty-nine years more, and I will probably be dead; nay, alive for evermore."

CHAPTER VI.

SOCIAL LIFE IN CALIFORNIA.

Social life indeed! Precious little of that article found or even tolerated in California for years. California was a vast social Sahara. The element of social life, to be sure, is inherent in our being, and has, perhaps, a more prominent and varied manifestation in human life, than any other principle essential to humanity. Its most appropriate sphere of manifestation is in the well ordered family. It gives vitality and felicity to connubial, paternal, maternal, and filial relationships. It constitutes the integral bond which unites the family together, the severance of which is as the lightning bolt entering a man's soul. The man or woman in whom this principle is dead is a misanthrope, and abides in darkness, uncheered by one ray of light or hope; loves neither father, nor mother, nor brother, nor sister, nor son, nor daughter; a miserable being all alone in the world. The man who has no appropriate object on which to exercise his social affections, is a Selkirk, standing on his lonely island, surrounded by an ocean waste, fit emblem of the deep, dark void of his own restless soul. Look, for example, even at Father Adam in Eden. A bran new creation, all beaming in untarnished glory, and by the Creator himself pronounced "good," spread out before him. But among the teeming millions of animated nature, all moving in their pristine strength and beauty, there was not found a helpmeet for poor Adam, though he sought one diligently. The Lord saw that he was in a bad state of single wretchedness and said, "It is not good that the man should be alone: I will make him a helpmeet for him." When Adam awoke from that "deep sleep," and set his eyes on an object worthy his love, the most beautiful creature he ever saw in his life, part of himself, for himself, and all his own, loving him, and waiting to be loved by him, his paradise was complete; and Father Adam has ten thousand sons in California to-day, any one of whom would be most happy to sleep such a sleep as that, and to have two ribs taken out, if need be, could he but wake up in possession of a helpmeet. Alas! poor fellows, they have often slept a "deep sleep," and dreamed something about extracted ribs, and waked but to stare out on their own isolated wretchedness.

The tearful adieus of fathers, and sons, and brothers, as they departed for California, told of the deep-gushing fountains of social sympathy and affection which swelled their hearts. For weeks afterward they gazed daily, with tearful interest, at the mementoes from loved ones, already painfully distant; but they had launched out on unexplored seas of wealth-seeking adventure, and must look ahead. Many were without moral quadrant, compass, or chart, but all had the telescope of manifest destiny, through which they could see in the distance the auriferous mountains. Dark clouds sometimes intercepted their vision, but their edges were so beautifully fringed by the sunshine of hope, that they only added grandeur to the scene. Each one felt as certain of getting there, and of "making his pile," as did the prophet Balaam, when trotting over to Mount Peor; but, poor fellows, how many of them, like the prophet, were "driven to the wall." Having reached the land of gold, and the flurry and surprises of the arrival over, then came the initiation of the "green horns," as they were familiarly called, into the mysteries of California life, which was a very interesting, and in many cases a very serious affair. Some meeting friends there, had but little difficulty; but many arrived destitute of both friends and funds. All, however, soon learned that to succeed in California, every man must be self-reliant and independent, a *brave* on his own account. Home reflections and associations brought painful contrasts to view, and led to gloomy forebodings, and must hence be dismissed from their minds.

Those who "put up at the hotel, at thirty dollars per week," found no soft beds in rosewood, with downy pillows, but occupied "bunks" made of rough boards, on the side of the wall, shelving one above another, as in emigrant ships. I have seen not only the walls of hotel lofts thus lined with bunks, but large cribs of them, extending up to the roof of the house, covering the entire floor, except narrow passages giving access to them. Sheets were a superfluity not indulged in; pillows were of straw; mattresses, where they had any, were of the same; but in many cases the sleeper lay on the board which held him up off his follow-sleeper beneath. I tried one night to sleep in one, which, unfortunately for me, was covered with cross slats, evidently designed for a mattress; but the last-mentioned very important article, in such a case, was not there. Turning and rolling on these slats, I longed for the morning. The soft side of a board, compared with them, would have been a luxury.

To the foregoing sleeping arrangements, if you add a few coarse gray blankets, you will have an original California lodging-house furnished. I heard it positively asserted by many, who had been made tremblingly sensible of the fact, that in some houses a few pair of blankets supplied a houseful of lodgers. As the weary fellows "turned in" one after another, they were comfortably covered till they would fall

CALIFORNIA LODGING-ROOM.

into a sound sleep, and then the blankets were removed to cover a new recruit, and thus they were passed round for the accommodation of the whole company. By way of variety, the adventurous lodgers in those pioneer hotels were frequently visited by the third plague of Egypt, accompanied by a liliputian host of the flea tribe, whose stimulating influence upon their subjects is represented in the accompanying cut. Any man who is not proof against fleas, or who cannot effect a good insurance on his skin, had better keep away from old Spanish towns and Indian villages. When I was at Valparaiso I preached for the Rev. Mr. Trumbull; spent an evening in his company, and heard him relate a little of his experience with fleas. Said he: "When I first came to this place I feared the fleas would worry the life out of me. I could neither eat nor sleep, nor stay awake with any comfort. But after a few weeks I got used to them, and now I pay no attention to them. The biting of a dozen at once don't cause me to wince, nor lift my pen from my paper."

Others, not willing to pay much for the mere name of "boarding at the hotel," formed mess-companies, pitched their own tent, bought a skillet and coffee-pot, and kept "bachelor's hall." This mode of life is familiarly known in California as "ranching." Their tent or cabin is called the "ranch," from "rancho," the Spanish name for a farm. A large proportion of the miners still live in this way. "Ranchers" usually cook by turns; sleep in bunks furnished with a pair of blankets, and a few old clothes; a pair of trowsers rolled up with an old coat, make a pretty good pillow. "Wash-day" among the ranchers comes but seldom, and is never welcome; for there are no wives, nor daughters, nor Bridgets to do the washing. In San Francisco, in 1849–50, there was but little washing done. Men had not yet learned how, and to have it done cost from six to nine dollars per dozen; so it was generally found cheaper to give their check-shirts a good wearing, (white was out of the question,) and then shed them off into the streets, and put on new ones. I have seen dozens of shirts lying around in the streets and vacant lots, which had thus been worn once and never washed. There were yet other fortune-seekers who, instead of ranching in companies, went alone. How they lived I know not; but they slept each in a home-made cot, at each end of which was a fork, driven into the ground, in which lay a ridge-pole, with just enough of canvas stretched over it to cover the cot. The cot, tent, and all were not four feet high. There was one of this kind during the winter of 1849–50 near where I lived on Jackson-street. In the morning I could see the fellow crawl out of his cot from under his little tent, sometimes head foremost; at other times his feet would first appear. While I have seen large tents carried before the blast, ridge-pole, rigging and all, this little tent, which looked like a covered grave, stood the storms of winter without moving a pin.

The various classes thus described are not made up of the isolated cases, but represent the great mass of the early denizens of the golden land; men who wore check-shirts, and gray or red flannel, instead of coats; trowsers, fastened up by a leather-girdle, such as was worn by John the Baptist, and they were planted down to their knees into the coarsest boots the market afforded. These were the men who, but a few months before, were known among their friends at home as doctors, lawyers, judges, and mechanics, clothed in broadcloth and fine linen, each one a center of social light and life, around which daily revolved the beautiful and gay, fair daughters, sisters, and wives. How did these men so soon become rustics in California? What has become of their polish and social life? I'll tell you. A large class of California adventurers thought about home, and mourned their absence from loved ones, till gloom and despair settled down on their souls. Hope died, energy and effort were paralyzed, and they became helpless and worthless. Some of this class moved round like specters a few months, and then managed to beg, or otherwise secure their passage home to their friends. Whether social life ever had a sound revival in them I know not.

There was one of this class with whom I was acquainted, who took a shipment of bonnets to California in 1849. There were very few American ladies in the country; the Spanish ladies wore no bonnets, so my friend P. found no sale for his bonnets. In vain he peddled them round among the men; no one wanted a bonnet. He had some money also, but knew not what to do with it. Once or twice a week he came to consult me as to what he had better do? Said I: "My dear fellow, you must go to work; you cannot long bear California expenses unless you draw upon California resources. Moreover, if you continue to mope about the streets you will take the blues so badly that you'll die; you must do something. If you can't open a large store, open a stand on the sidewalk until you can do better; if you can't do that, go to work on the streets, roll a wheel-barrow at four dollars per day."

"I can't work on the streets," said he; "I've always been accustomed to merchandising, and can't do manual labor; but I must go into business."

"Very well," said I; "seek an opening to-day, and go at it."

Some time after this, as I passed down Commercial-street, I saw Mr. P. striding diagonally across the street to meet me. His face seemed much elongated, and I expected to hear a sad tale. Approaching me he said:

"Mr. Taylor, what shall I do?" choking with an agony of emotion.

"What's the matter now, Mr. P.?"

"O," said he, "I loaned my money to my messmate. He said he wanted it but a few days, till I got ready to go into business, and now he's got my money and gone. I shall never see him again!"

"Well, Mr. P.," I replied, "I'm very sorry for you; but it's no use to mourn over lost money any more than over spilled milk. There's Captain Wooley, whom I know well, who made a thousand dollars, and one day last week as he was leaving his ship he put his purse containing his one thousand dollars in gold dust into his pocket; but poor fellow, he has no wife with him to sew up the holes in his pocket, so as he was descending his ship's ladder his purse, gold and all, slipped through a hole in his pocket into the bay. Well, sir, the captain said he never looked back, nor lost one minute grieving over it. He knew it was gone, and just went to work with great purpose of heart to make another thousand. And yesterday as I walked out on Montgomery-street, a man called me by name: 'Mr. Taylor, look here; I made five thousand dollars, and had it hid away in my shanty here, and last night some rascal came and stole every dollar of it; so I'm just where I started. But never mind,' continued he; 'I'll go to work and make five thousand more, and will try and put it where the rogues can't get hold of it.' And Mr. E., a friend of mine, who boarded up town, went down one morning to his auction store, which he had just filled with goods on his own account, but lo! the store, goods and all were gone! While he slept the whole were consumed by fire. Did he stop to mourn over his losses? No, sir; he got another place, and went into business before the setting of that day's sun. And here are hundreds of men who had made a fortune, and had it all invested in their storehouses and the goods that filled them, and in a single night the dreadful fires we have had have laid them all in ashes. Well, sir, in the midst of smoke and ruins a new store, phœnix like, springs right up, and is filled with goods by the time the smoke of their former fortunes has cleared away. So you see, Mr. P., if you would get along in California you must pick up courage and go to work, and stick to it till success crowns your patient toil."

Mr. P. soon afterward returned home, where he should have stayed in the first place.

Another of this class came often to me to know "what he must do to be saved" *from starvation?* So I said to him one day:

"Mr. L., a wag was once asked, 'How many dog days are there?' His prompt reply was, 'Every dog has his day.' Now, Mr. L., if you'll go to work, and be patient, I think you'll have your day in California, as well as others."

He afterward succeeded much better, and attributed his success mainly to that little piece of advice. But a great many of this class in their despondency gave up, and sought comfort in the intoxicating bowl, and went down to infamy and death. As I walked over the sand hills back of the city of San Francisco, I found Simon S. lying under a scrub oak, in rags, reduced by drunkenness and disease to the verge of the grave. As I exhorted him to give up strong drink, seek religion, go to work, and become a man, O how bitterly he wept; but, poor fellow, energy was gone, hope had fled, nothing left to stimulate an effort.

H. S., a fine business man, with an interesting young wife and child in the city of B., was taken from the gutter by his friends again and again. They knew him at home and loved him, and greatly desired to save him, but finally, during one of those dreadful nights of storm and tempest in San Francisco, in the winter of 1849, he was picked up by the police, and put into a station-house on the Plaza for protection from the rain; and in the morning, when they went to wake him up, they found him cold in death. I need not multiply the notices of such cases, as I have seen them by hundreds by the waysides and in the hospitals. Their "name is legion."

There was another large class of California adventurers, who, retaining their social life, and hope, and energy, tried to substitute objects of social affection for the wives, sisters, and daughters they could not see. These substitutes consisted of pet dogs, cats, etc. A company of men ranching near where I lived on Jackson-street, had at one time a couple of grizzly bears, with which they spent their social hours. A pet coon made a pretty good companion for some, others preferred a caged wild cat, or California lion. One man, whom I used to see often, had a large family which accompanied him wherever he went. His family consisted of a bay horse, two dogs, two sheep, and two goats. Whenever I met one of that circle (and they were often seen in the streets) I saw them all together, and they seemed to be a very harmonious family indeed. Now these animals seemed to be very mean substitutes for families "at home," but, poor fellows, what better could they do?

But again, the largest class of wealth seekers in California seemed to ignore their social nature, and substitute for it California excitement. The social element of their souls seemed to be absorbed by raging thirst for gain, an excitement that burned with quenchless glow. The stimulants to excitement may be classed as ordinary and extraordinary. Among the ordinary were the daily excitements of business. Enormous prices and wages; "happy hits and large strikes;" "big lumps and rich diggings found;" fortunes made and lost; these constituted the themes of every-day talk, attended by a vast amount of bluster and patient toil.

The day's work and supper over, and what next? "Sit down in that dirty ranch and think about home? Never! I'd take the blues in an hour, and be worthless for a week. Must have some entertainment." "Where? At some friend's social fireside." "No such thing to be found within five thousand miles. Too far for this evening. Come, boys, let's take a walk down town." They soon come to a drinking saloon splendidly ornamented and illuminated, and behind the bar a beautiful-looking woman. They stop and glance at her a moment, and think of sisters and fair loves at home. "She's a confounded pretty girl, ain't she, Bill?" "She is, indeed; let's take a drink, and we'll get a good look at her." So they refresh their spirits at the bar. They next come to a gambling saloon, fitted up like a palace. From a stage in the rear end of the magnificent saloon, a band of the sweetest music sends forth its melody on the gentle stillness of summer's evening. In a front corner is a bar, where the *needful* is displayed in all its deceptive and deadly varieties. From front to rear the tables are laden with gold, and crowding hundreds of every nation fill the aisles, both as spectators and participators. "One evening sixteen thousand dollars' worth of gold dust was laid upon a faro table as a bet. This was lost by the keeper of the table, who counted out the money to the winner without a murmur, and continued his business with a cheerful countenance, and apparently with as good spirits as though he had incurred no more than an ordinary loss. As high as twenty thousand dollars, it is said, have been risked upon the turn of a card. Five thousand, three thousand, and one thousand were repeatedly ventured. The ordinary stakes, however, were by no means so high as these sums, from fifty cents to five dollars being the usual amount; and thus the common day laborer could lay his moderate stake as stylishly as a lord."—*Annals of San Francisco*, p. 249.

There, too, were beautiful women, dressed in silk and satin, lending enchantment to the scene, and enticing the unwary to the game. A little further on was "the house of the strange woman," magnificent without, beautiful within, furnished with Brussels, velvet, silk, and damask. Heavy furniture of rosewood, and walls hung with beautiful paintings; and music from pianoforte, melodeon, and harp; no house more prominent or beautiful for situation in the city. The mistress, beautified by all the magic touches of art, rode fast horses, promenaded the streets, enticed many by "her much fair speech," who went "after her straightway, as an ox goeth to the slaughter, or as a fool to the correction of the stocks."

The most of the virtuous women in California in early days had to look after their children and attend to housework, not generally being able to pay one hundred dollars per month for a servant to help them, and hence could not contribute much to the social life of the country. Thus virtue plodded through the streets, bearing burdens, while prostitutes, lauded and caressed, became the leading conservators of social life, fanning its waning fires into ephemeral brightness by a magnificent display of their presence and deceitful smiles.

To show how the devil of licentiousness had encoiled himself under the foundations of society, and held in his deadly fangs its very vitals, we quote the following life-scene from the "*Annals of San Francisco*:"

"See yonder house. Its curtains are of the purest white lace, embroidered, and crimson damask. All the fixtures are in keeping, most expensive, most voluptuous, most gorgeous; the favorite ones with the same class of humanity, whose dress and decorations have been made so significant ever since the name of their city and trade, 'Babylon.' It is *soirée* night. The 'lady' of the establishment has sent most polite invitations, got up on the finest and most beautifully embossed note-paper, to all the principal gentlemen of the city, including collector of the port, mayor, aldermen, judges of the county, and members of the Legislature. A splendid band of music is in attendance. Away over the Turkey or Brussels carpet whirls the politician with some sparkling beauty, as fair as frail; and the judge joins in and enjoys the dance in company with the beautiful but lost beings whom to-morrow he may send to the house of correction. Everything is conducted with the utmost propriety. Not an unbecoming word is heard, not an objectionable action seen. The girls are on their good behavior, and are proud once more to move, and act, and appear as ladies. Did you not know, you would not suspect that you were in one of those dreadful places so vividly described by Solomon; and were it not for the great proportion of beauty present, you might suppose yourself in a saloon of upper-tendom.

"But the dance is over; now for the supper-table. Everything within the bounds of the market and the skill of the cook and confectioner is before you. Opposite, and by your side, that which nor cook nor confectioner's skill have made what they are, cheeks where the ravages of dissipation have been skillfully hidden, and eyes with pristine brilliancy undimmed, or even heightened by the spirit of the recent champagne. And here the illusion fades. The champagne alone is paid for. The *soirée* has cost the mistress one thousand dollars; and at the supper, and during the night, she sells twelve dozen of champaigne at ten dollars a bottle! This is a literal fact, not an idea, nor a draft upon the imagination, decorated with the colors of fancy."—Pp. 668, 669.

This horrible picture, said to be truthfully drawn from real life, and from what I have seen outside, I have no reason to doubt it, tells a sad tale; but, thank the Lord, "Babylon has fallen! has fallen!" and now above its scattered ruins the walls of the temple of virtue are towering, clearly defined in the sunshine of a better day, and already exhibiting permanence, beauty, and grandeur, and still going up and hastening on to a glorious consummation. Men and women of sterling integrity and purity steadily withstood the desolating tide of licentiousness that swept over the land, often at the hazard of life, some falling in the struggle by the assassin's hand, until gambling was successfully put down by law throughout the state, and sunk under the odium of outraged public feeling, a thousand per cent. below par, and the whole fraternity of the "strange woman" has shared about the same fate.

Sunday amusements held a very prominent place among the entertainments of early days in California; consisting in horse-racing, bull-baiting, an occasional fight between a mad bull and a man, and more frequently between a bull and a grizzly bear. The race-tracks, and first grand Sunday resort of San

Franciscans, was at "Mission Doloros," about two miles from the city. There are now two plank roads leading to the mission, and omnibuses running every half hour. Several thousands of persons on a single Sunday sometimes visited it, to witness one or more of the scenes described. "Russ' Garden," about half way out on the mission road, which contains a large circular hall for the accommodation of pleasure-seeking parties, is a great rendezvous for Sabbath breakers, especially among the Germans. Bands of music, fiddling, dancing, singing, feasting, and drinking constitute the principal entertainment there. The city of Oakland, across the bay, eight miles distant from San Francisco, became the rival of "Mission Dolores" in Sunday amusements. One day, in crossing the bay in the Oakland "steamer Clinton," I saw a man posting on the side of the wheelhouse the following bill, in large letters: "Great bear fight, in front of the American Hotel, in Oakland, between the red bear Sampson, and a large Grizzly, on Sunday, January 29, 1854. The steamer Clinton will make two extra trips for the accommodation of the public."

"On Sunday?" inquired one of the uninitiated, who had recently arrived.

"O yes," replied an intelligent-looking Englishman; "Sunday's a great day; a great day here in California."

CITY OF OAKLAND.

"Nothing could be done," said the poster, "on a week-day."

"O no," answered the Englishman, "if I were to have anything of the sort, I would certainly have it on Sunday; may just as well go to hell on Sunday as on any other day; all going there anyhow. I look at the thing philosophically."

Another then added: "We are not burdened with religion here in California."

"The fact is," said the poster, "religion won't pay here in California."

I consider this, in regard to the whole Sabbath-breaking fraternity, as a fair specimen of California ethics.

In connection with bull-baiting, bear-fighting, etc., we had, by way of variety, a duel occasionally, in which an editor or politician was sometimes killed, as were the bulls and bears, in the presence of the excited multitude.

CHAPTER VII.

SOCIAL LIFE—CONTINUED.

In the early history of California cities and towns no Sabbath was recognized in merchandise and trade; and those who observed it at all observed it only as a holiday, the day for a "grand bust up," or for gunning, or a dancing party, or an excursion party, or some of the varieties before mentioned.

I once called on a Roman Catholic in San Francisco for a subscription for a Methodist church: "O yes," said he, "I'll give you a hundred dollars; I'm a Catholic, but I see the great advantages of churches in a community like this. I remember when nothing could be seen in this city on Sunday but the bustle of business, and nothing heard but the rattle of horse-hoofs, and the shouts of those engaged in or witnessing the race. But since churches have been erected, and the preaching of the Gospel introduced, Sabbath is fast becoming a quiet day; respectable business houses are closed, and horse-racing has been driven beyond the limits of the city. I go in for the multiplication of churches as the best means of improving society."

The embarcation of Sunday excursion parties, accompanied by a band of music, drew thousands of persons to the wharf to hear the music, and witness their departure. I frequently took advantage of such occasions, by taking my stand in sight and hearing, and when the boat's hawsers were cast off, would strike up a loud song, and draw the returning crowd, and sound in their ears the tocsin of the coming judgments of a sin-avenging God, and present them with an offer of mercy through the Crucified. The excitement of such occasions afforded a fine opportunity of driving some strong appeals to the sinner's conscience.

On one such occasion, just as I had sung up the crowd, a dog-fight occurred in the street fronting the next block, and a large part of my audience ran to see the fight, so that the programme of that morning's excitants would stand thus: first, the excursion and music; second, the songs of the preacher; third, the dog-fight; and fourth, another song from the preacher, which drew the audience back as soon as the dogs had finished their part. I then said to them, by way of introduction: "Gentlemen, if I could come to you this morning and say, Ho! all ye who want to go to heaven, now's your time. A splendid line of celestial steamers will run, for a few days, from San Francisco to the port of Glory, a country every way superior to California, having in it the richest gold diggings ever discovered, the very streets of the great city being paved with gold. In that country are oceans of lager beer and drinks of every kind, and all free; pretty women also, and pleasures in endless variety, exceeding the dreams of Mohammed as far as the brightness of the meridian sun exceeds the dim twinkle of the glow-worm! Programme for the voyage: Embarcation amid the melody of the best band in the world. That music which so attracted you this morning not to be mentioned in the comparison. Appropriate entertainments for each week day, to be announced daily. Each Sunday to be celebrated, first, with a grand feast, closing with a rich profusion of lager beer, champagne, good old port, whisky punch, brandy-smashes, Cogniac, hot Tom and Jerry, etc. Second, a game at cards. Third, a grand ball in the upper saloon. Fourth, a dog-fight on the upper deck. Fifth, a theatrical performance in the evening, closing with a magnificent farce. O my friends and fellow-citizens, if I could truthfully publish such an advertisement as that, I think about two sermons on the Plaza would suffice to convert the whole city, except some of those croakers who are always talking about death, hell, and judgment, and we would all quit this lower world of trouble, and take the steamer for heaven on her next trip."

By that time I could bid defiance to all the dogs

in town. I had the crowd, and, perhaps, never gave a set of men a more faithful warning in my life. It turned out to be a very solemn and tearful meeting.

The first steamboat built in California was called the "Sagamore." On the 29th of October, 1850, the admission of California as a state into the Union, was celebrated by grand processions of various public bodies, and the people generally, Americans, French, Italians, Chinese, etc., with the best of music and the thunder of heavy ordnance, and the fizzing and popping of fire-crackers, barrels of which were burned by the Chinamen. When all assembled on the Plaza, an oration was delivered by Judge Bennett, of the Supreme Court. One of the incidents of that day was the explosion of this first California built steamer, the Sagamore. Just after leaving the wharf for Stockton, with a load of merry souls who had been participating in the common joy, her boiler burst and broke to fragments all her top works from stem to stern. It was believed that between thirty and forty persons were killed. I witnessed that tragedy, and tried to minister to the dying. Its details were horrible. I saw a man named Johnson, from Illinois, where he had a wife and two children, brought ashore with one leg torn off at the calf. He thought he would recover, but died in fifteen minutes. He had a brother-in-law who died as he was being carried into the house where the other was dying. Another died as they brought him ashore. I saw a weeping Spanish woman, holding on her lap a man whose head had been split open, and his brains lay scattered on the wharf. Many more, badly wounded and burned, were taken to the hospital. (See Seven Years' Street-Preaching, etc., p. 90.)

One poor fellow, with a broken leg, implored them not to take him to a hospital, saying, "For mercy sake, don't take me to a hospital, or I shall die. Take me to a good hotel, and employ a good physician to attend on me. I've got plenty of money, and will pay for everything that is done for me."

Philip Groves, the shouting Methodist, was aboard in the midst of the explosion, and as he crawled up from under the broken timbers, he shouted, "Halleluiah! I am ready! Glory be to God, I'm all right!" On examination he found that he was not hurt; but his hat, containing some valuable papers, was gone. By and by a man came to him in the crowd, and said:

"Is this your hat, sir?"

"Yes, sir."

His papers were all safe, as he left them. He never knew how his hat got ashore, unless it was blown on the wharf by the explosion.

A Swedish sailor said to me the next day: "When the Sagamore was launched and fitted up, the captain invited everybody who wanted to break the

Sabbath to come and take a Sunday trip in her. Her first run was for a Sunday excursion; God was displeased, and now we see what it has come to." The wreck was re-fitted, and called the "The Boston." For a time she was used principally as a Sunday excursion boat. On one occasion they moored her near our Bethel Ship. Mrs. Taylor happened to be on deck when they were "making fast" to our ship, and said to the captain, "I wish you would not tie that Sabbath-breaker to our Bethel. I am afraid of her. I am daily expecting to see her explode, or take fire and burn up." Not long after she took fire across the bay, near Oakland, where her keel still lies embedded in the mud. A great many mishaps attended those Sunday excursions.

"Spanish fandangoes" (a rude native dance) were very common in the early days of California. Fancy dress balls and masquerades soon came in vogue, and then followed the establishment of theaters, and an ever-changing variety of entertainments for the excited masses. In the mines, to this day, there are itinerant theatricals, minstrels, circuses, performers in legerdemain, dog and monkey shows, etc., constantly traveling to and fro, entertaining the miners at a dollar per head. I had a good deal of competition with these during a preaching tour I made through the mines in 1855. At Springfield they had too much music for me, and left me but a small audience to preach to. At Shaw's Flat they had to wait till I had done preaching before they could get the crowd; so also at Smith's Flat they waited quietly till I dismissed my audience, and then tuned up. I heard many say, after preaching at the last-named place, "I'll save my dollar to-night sure."

I am no apologist for the moral degeneracy and ruin of thousands in California; but, in the light of the foregoing facts, it is easy to see how insidiously the foe insnared them. It is not at all remarkable that many fell. Among the excitements extraordinary may be named grand political gatherings and celebrations, a sweeping fire occasionally, vigilance committees, and the mass-meetings called together under the administration of Judge Lynch.

Some idea of such exciting occasions may be gathered from the accompanying cut, which represents a scene enacted at the City Hall in San Francisco, February 22, 1851. On the nineteenth of that month the store of C. J. Jansen & Co. was entered about eight o'clock P. M. by two men, who said they wanted to buy blankets. As Mr. Jansen, who was in the store alone, turned to get the articles, he was knocked senseless to the floor with a "slung shot." The premises were robbed of two thousand dollars, and the rogues fled. Two men, Windred and Burdue, were next day arrested on suspicion and lodged in jail under the City Hall. By the twenty-first

CITY HALL ON FEBRUARY 22, 1851.

Jansen had so far recovered as to be able to give testimony, and, with but a shade of doubt, identified the two men under arrest as the robbers of the store. The frequent occurrence of such outrages, and the general belief that there was a large organized band of robbers and murderers confederated throughout the state, led to a popular outburst of vengeance, and a demand for the prisoners by a crowd of eight thousand persons. At the request of Windred's wife, I with great difficulty pressed my way through the excited mass, and visited the prisoners. Above the din and commotion of the multitude the shouts resounded from every direction, "Have them out! hang them!" "The courts are sure to let them go!" "Hang them now!" I spent some time with the prisoners, as they were expecting every minute to be dragged out and hung.

After a few hours, on certain assurances from leading city authorities that the prisoners should be promptly tried and justly dealt with, the crowd dispersed.

Windred afterward broke jail and ran away. Burdue was convicted, and sent to Marysville to be tried for the murder of Mr. Moore, sheriff of Auburn, and was there convicted and sentenced to be hung; but pending this sentence the San Francisco Vigilance Committee arrested the real murderer and robber for whom Burdue, from exact personal appearance, had

12

been mistaken; so Burdue was afterward released, and the guilty man hung.

I was walking down Pacific wharf one Saturday afternoon, in company with Rev. S. D. Simonds, when we saw aboard the clipper ship "Challenge," which had just come into port, a vast crowd of men. We supposed that they had come to see the splendid ship, and I remarked: "Brother Simonds, the deck of that ship will be a good place for me to preach to-morrow. If hundreds come to see her in the week, there will be thousands on Sunday, and I'll have an opportunity of preaching the Gospel to them."

"Good," said he; "we'll go aboard and get permission of the captain."

So we went aboard, and hunted from cabin to forecastle and back again, but could find no captain. We soon learned that all the rest were hunting the captain too.

"Why, what's the matter here?" said I.

"Matter enough," replied one; "Captain W. has killed several of his crew; and if you'll look into the forecastle you'll see such a battered up set of men as you never saw before."

"We're after the captain," responded one and another. "We'll hang him to the yard-arm!"

The object of our search being so different from that of the crowd, we suddenly left.

It was said that the captain had an octagon shaped

stick, about four feet long, which he called his "persuader," and his persuasions were so earnest that several men died under the force of them. He, however, evaded the search of the exasperated crowd, concealed himself till the people were all drawn off by some other extraordinary excitement, and then came forward, stood his trial in court, and was acquitted.

Another class of extraordinary excitements grew out of the wonderful gold discoveries that were continually being made, such as "Gold Lake," "Gold Bluffs," "Australian Gold Fields," "Kern River Diggings," etc. The papers were filled with the wonderful tidings, ships were chartered, caravans formed, men by thousands would leave their business of whatever kind, and away to make their *pile* at once, without any further delay.

The following account of the "Gold Bluff" excitement we extract from the "Annals of San Francisco:"

"*January*, 1851.—San Francisco has been startled 'from its propriety' by news from the celebrated 'Gold Bluffs,' and during the greater part of this month has dreamed unutterable things of black sand, and gray sand, and cargoes of gold. A band of pioneers and prospecters had recently proceeded in the 'Chesapeake' steamer northward to the Klamath River, near which, on the sea-shore, they fancied they had found the richest and most extraordinary gold field that had ever been known. The sands of the sea, for a broad space several miles in length, beneath cliffs some hundreds of feet high, appeared to be literally composed in one half at least of the pure metal. Millions of diggers for ages to come could not exhaust that grand deposit. Already a few miners had collected about the spot; but these were so amazed and lost in the midst of the surrounding treasure that they knew not what to do. No man could carry more than seventy-five or a hundred pounds weight upon his back for any great distance; and with that quantity of pure gold it was ridiculous, so it was, to be content when numberless tons lay about. A brilliant reporter for the *Alta California* says: 'The gold is mixed with black sand, in proportions of from ten cents to ten dollars the pound. At times when the surf is high the gold is not easily discovered; but in the spring of the year, after a succession of calms, the entire beach is covered with bright and yellow gold. Mr. Collins, the secretary of the Pacific Mining Company, measured a patch of gold and sand, and estimates it will yield to each member of the company the snug little sum of $43,-000,000, (*say* forty-three *millions* of dollars,) and the estimate is formed upon a calculation that the sand holds out to be one tenth as rich as observation warrants them in supposing.'

"No digging even was required, since one had only to stoop a little, and raise as much as he wished of the stuff—half gold, half sand—from the surface of the beach. Back the adventurers hastened to San Francisco, where they had long been impatiently expected, and the glorious news ran like wild-fire among the people.

"General John Wilson and Mr. John A. Collins, both of whom had been among the number of discoverers, frankly testified to the truth of these wonderful statements. The beach, they said, for a great distance, was literally strewed with pure gold. It was found in the greatest quantity in a certain kind of 'black sand,' although the 'gray sand,' which was rather more abundant, contained likewise a large proportion of the same black-colored stuff, with its special share of gold. 'Mr. Collins,' says the poetic reporter, 'saw a man who had accumulated fifty thousand pounds, or fifty tons, he did not recollect which, of the richest kind of black sand.

"Such intelligence astounded the community. In a few days eight vessels were announced as about to sail for this extraordinary region. The magic phrase 'Gold Bluffs! Gold Bluffs!' everywhere startled the most apathetic, and aroused him as with a galvanic shock. 'Gold Bluffs!' filled the columns of newspapers among the shipping advertisements; they covered, on huge posters, the blank walls of houses at the corners of the streets; they were in every man's mouth. A company was formed, called the 'Pacific Mining Company,' the shares of which instantly rose to a handsome premium. There seemed no doubt of their incalculable gains, since they showed numerous samples of the wondrous 'black sand,' where the golden particles lay and shone mildly as stars in the milky way innumerable. The company had already, by the greatest good fortune, secured a considerable number of miners' claims, embracing indeed the entire beach beneath the 'bluffs,' so that all was clear for immediate operations.

"The first damper to the hot blast that raged through the town, and from whence it spread and fired up distant countries, until the arrival of the next mail, was intelligence from the earliest miners, that they found it very difficult to separate first the black sand from the gray, and next the gold itself from the black sand, the particles of the precious metal being so remarkably fine. A little later it was found that the innumerable "patches" of black sand began most unaccountably to disappear. Heavy seas came and swept them right away; and though it was hoped that heavier seas might soon bring them back again, the people got tired waiting for that event, and hastily fled from the place, ashamed of their hopes and credulity. Much serious loss was suffered by the '*Gold Bluffs*' piece of business.

"The unfortunate 'Pacific Mining Company' had bought the *Chesapeake*, at a cost, for boat and repairs, of *twenty thousand dollars;* had run her up the coast several trips at the loss of as many thousand more; and afterward, when she had been injured in a storm, were glad to sell her for about two thousand dollars.

"There was considerable gold at the *Bluffs*, but it turned out in the end to cost more trouble to gather than it was worth. Hence the place was abandoned, except by a few still hopeful individuals, after a few months' trial."—Pp. 311–314.

Dr. H., a friend of mine, a very tall man from Missouri, was carried off by the "Gold Bluff" fever. When nearly ready to sail, he said to me: "Mr. Taylor, they tell me that I can easily make there eleven hundred dollars per day; but you know I'm not easily moved by such reports, [moving then under a high pressure of excited hope at the rate of six knots per hour.] I shall be satisfied," continued he, "if I make three hundred dollars per day, and that I know I can do without any difficulty."

A few months afterward the doctor returned to San Francisco almost in rags, out of money, and as lean as a pelican in the wilderness. He told me a sad story of his adventures, reverses, and sufferings. He had lost his all, had been shipwrecked, put on short allowance of water and food, and had nearly starved to death.

But though social life, as I have shown by the facts and illustrations under this head, was in many quenched by the tide of their reverses and sorrows; in many more ignored and superseded by the grasping spirit of the times and the excitements of the country; and though by others prostituted and abused, there always have been occasions when the springs of social life in California suddenly broke out afresh, like mountain rills after a thunder shower, and flowed, for a short season, with astonishing impetuosity.

The monthly, and afterward semi-monthly, arrival of the mails, with letters from home, generally sufficed to open the fountains of social sympathy in the souls of the multiplied thousands of isolated wanderers scattered over the land. I took with me from Baltimore a large package of letters, round Cape Horn, from friends to their friends in California.

At that time but few persons seemed to realize that there was anything of California outside of San Francisco, and my going there was thought to afford the surest means of a safe conveyance of letters; for I would, of course, meet all their friends on my arrival, see them face to face, and deliver the letters in person. The said friends, however, were scattered possibly back through the mountains, and along the coast, from San Diego to Puget Sound, a

THE POST-OFFICE, CORNER OF PIKE AND CLAY STREETS.

distance of more than a thousand miles, many of whom I never met in seven years.

I met with Joseph Stocker, a good Baltimore friend of mine, a few months after my arrival, and handed him a letter from his wife. He had not seen her for nearly a year, and in all that time had not received a letter from home. He broke the long-expected letter, and its effect upon him was wonderful. It did not jerk him out of his boots, exactly, but it did more; contrary to all his plans, and at a cost of immense sacrifice of business interests, it carried him, boots and all, out of the territory by the next steamer. I doubt if he indulged in the luxury of one good night's rest until he saw his wife and children. He soon after returned to California accompanied by his good wife and babes.

The slow single file marches in front of the Post-office, to the windows of delivery, by long lines of anxious faces, formed several hours before the opening of the office, furnished evidence of the social longings of their hearts. It was interesting to mark the countenances and conduct of men as they turned away from the delivery windows at the horrible announcement, "Nothing for you, sir," or as they grasped and broke open the letters which brought them news from home. (California Post-office scenes are described at length in my "Seven Years' Street Preaching," etc., p. 282.)

But what contributed still more to revive and promote social life in California was the semi-monthly arrival of families. For a couple of years after the gold discovery but very few of the great mass of California adventurers had any thought of a permanent settlement in that country. They had generally given themselves about two years in which to make their "pile," and return home. They therefore cared nothing about California except for her gold, and hence felt but little responsibility in regard to their conduct or character. Indeed very many had left their character at home, if they had any, as an old Missouri sinner said he left his religion. Said he: "I knew I couldn't carry my religion with me through California, so when I left home in Missouri I hung my religious cloak on my gate-post until I should return."

After a couple of years' sojourn in California, very many began seriously to contemplate a permanent settlement in that country. They were delighted with the climate, and became deeply interested in the development of the immense resources of the country, agricultural, mineral, and commercial, and in the growing greatness of their young giant state. Then such expressions as these became very common: "If I had my family here I never would leave California; but I can't consent to bring my family to such a place. Everything is inviting, so far as the country, physically, is concerned; but the social and moral condition of the people is so horribly bad, I can't risk the education of my children in such a place." Very many found, too, at the end of their two years, that they had done nearly everything else but "make their pile," and could not bear the mortification of returning without it; but having a fine prospect ahead, they were led at once to say: "O if I had my family here, and could settle down and take my time at it, I would make my fortune and live at ease in this most delightful climate in the world; but O, the moral and social condition of the country is horrible!" These and similar considerations, together with the fact that some families had been there from the first, and got along pleasantly, wife and children healthful and happy, led men by the hundred to the determination to go or send for their families, and make a home in California.

As soon as they made up their minds to settle permanently in the country, their conduct underwent a great change for the better. They began earnestly to manifest interest in the establishment of schools and churches, the regular preaching of the Gospel, the better observance of the Sabbath, and whatever they thought would contribute to improve the social condition of society. Some, who could leave their business, went in person for their families; but many more, not being able to leave without too great a sacrifice of time or money, sent for their families. Single men, also, from similar considerations, came to similar conclusions in regard to permanent settlement. Some, having matrimonial engagements at home, began to arrange for their consummation with reference to a home in California. Others determined to live in California at any rate, and trust to getting a wife to share their fortunes, either from home or by good fortune from among the arrivals of fair ones, or from the divorcement or death of some fellow who had a wife in California. A great many young men have modestly but seriously requested my observation to find out, and my mediation to try and secure for them each a good wife. I once received a letter from a stranger, whom I had never seen, living in Badego Valley, to this effect:

"Dear Sir,—You will please pardon the liberty I take in addressing to you this note, and especially for introducing the subject it contains.

"I am a young man, twenty-nine years old, five feet ten inches high, possessing a sound constitution and good health; I have a good farm, well stocked, well improved, and all paid for. I want to make this my home; but I am a single man, living alone, but I find it not good to be alone, and I want a wife. I thought, as you always take an interest in every good work, and as you live in that great port of entry, you might be kind enough to recommend to me some lady who would make me a good wife. I would like to have one possessing good common sense, good disposition, and one who understands how to attend to household duties. I think I could make such a woman happy, and should not expect her to work beyond her own inclination. I am not very particular about beauty, nor whether she has a cent of money. If you can render me any service in this matter, I shall be exceedingly obliged, and will, besides, remunerate you handsomely for your trouble. Please write me at your earliest convenience.

"Yours respectfully."

His proper signature and address were added, but, poor fellow, the demand was so great among my intimate acquaintances, and the supply so limited, that I could do nothing for him. If it had been practicable for a man to have opened an "intelligence office," with a good supply of wives instead of servants, he would have had a run almost equal to the run on the banks in Wall-street a few months ago.

Mr. S., a friend of mine, in the city of Sonora, negotiated for a wife, through a very respectable married lady in that city, to whom he was well and favorably known. The said lady had a niece in the East, who she thought would suit, and be well suited in my friend Mr. S. So it was agreed that

Mr. S. should write the said young lady, proposing marriage, and the offer of money to pay her passage to California, and accompany the letter with his daguerreotype, and that the aunt should also write giving all necessary information, etc. The young lady was requested to answer at her earliest convenience, and, if she acceded to the proposition, to accompany her acceptance with her daguerreotype. It seemed that the young lady had been desiring to go to California to *see her aunt* for a long time, and on receiving such news from a far country, made up her mind to go without delay.

The next mail carried back her consent, and the likeness of her smiling face, and as soon as the passage-money could be sent from her unseen lover, she embarked for California. The two lovers were introduced to each other, and united together in the holy bands of matrimony, in the house of the aunt. I learn that they are getting along very pleasantly, and are perfectly delighted with each other.

If those humane societies now engaged in sending Eastern girls to the West as servants, could find it practicable to enlarge their business so as to send good girls of unblemished, certified character, to California for wives, I think it likely that a bachelor's fund could be raised in California, which would defray all the extra expense involved in the new department of the business. The thing would, of course, have to be judiciously managed, and not connected with "bloomer fashions" and "women's rights," as was an attempted enterprise of this kind a few years ago. They should go in care of good families, letting the bachelor subscribers, and the said families, alone know who they are, or where to be found after their arrival.

I merely throw this out as a suggestion, without stopping to mature, or to present any definite plan. It is, however, a subject of great importance. There are thousands of young men in California who, in their isolation, are going to ruin, who could be saved, and elevated to honorable citizenship, by the surplus of young ladies in the Eastern states who are worthy of good husbands.

The Mexican war and the gold attractions of California, have drawn away so many thousands of young men from the Eastern states, that the over proportion of young ladies on this side of the continent equals, and perhaps greatly exceeds the over proportion of young men in California, and their separation is a great social, moral, and national evil, which ought, if possible, to be remedied.

There were in California, according to the state census returns in 1856, in a total aggregate population of five hundred and seven thousand and sixty-seven, but seventy thousand white females all told; while there were one hundred and seventy-five thousand "men of war," men liable to military duty, between the ages of eighteen and forty-five.

Now, in view of the foregoing facts, it is not difficult to conceive of the thrilling social effect of a semi-monthly arrival in San Francisco of wives, families, and charming, virtuous Marys. An observer could always tell a month in advance when a man was expecting the arrival of his real or intended wife; the old slouch hat, check shirt, and coarse outer garments disappeared, and the gentleman could be seen on Sunday going to church, newly rigged from head to foot, with fine beaver or silk hat, white linen nice and clean, good broadcloth coat, velvet vest, patent-leather boots, his long beard shaven or neatly shorn, he looked like a new man. As the time drew near many of his hours were spent about the wharves or on telegraph hill, and every five minutes he was looking for the signal to announce the coming of the steamer. If, owing to some breakage or wreck there was a delay of a week or two, then the suspense was awful beyond description. I remember how my good friend Hon. D. O. Shattuck, Judge of the Superior Court of San Francisco, who was awaiting the arrival of his family on the steamer "North America," was agonized when he heard of the wreck of that steamer sixty miles below Acapulco. After much delay and suffering, however, they arrived in safety.

ARRIVAL OF A STEAMSHIP.

When the signal-flag on telegraph hill, announcing the arrival of a steamer, was thrown to the breeze, there was a general rush, and before the arrival gun was fired the wharf was crowded with such men as we have described, accompanied by those who sympathized socially with them, to the number sometimes of from three to five thousand.

The crowds became so great, and so annoying to passengers by their perfect blockade of the wharf and streets, that the two steamship companies put up a gate at the head of each of their wharves to prevent the assemblage of such masses, and gave strict orders to the gate-keepers to let none pass in unless they had families or friends aboard. But even after that enough had families or wives in anticipation, or particular friends aboard, to crowd the wharves still. The fact is, men by hundreds assembled through social sympathy to witness the happy greeting of men and their wives who had not seen each other for years, accompanied by dancing and shouting for joy, embracing, kissing, laughing, and crying, all to the great amusement of the excited throng. The disappointment of those whose wives did not arrive at the time expected was almost like a thunder shock. I knew a man well who boarded a steamer expecting to meet his wife, and the disappointment threw him into a spell of sickness, from which he did not recover for nearly a fortnight.

I knew another who came from the mines to meet his wife, waited several days in San Francisco for the arrival of the steamer, and then, instead of meeting his wife, he received a letter from her stating that she feared to make the voyage, and had indefinitely postponed it unless he would come home to accompany her. The poor man became almost deranged, now weeping with grief, now enraged, saying: "I'll never send for her again, and I'll never go home as long as I live! If she can get along without me I can get along without her. I'll go back to the mines, and live and die a hermit." Then after a pause he would add: "But there are my children; I can't bear to give them up! I don't know what to do, upon my soul I can't tell what to do!"

I took the poor fellow to my house, and reasoned with him on the subject until I succeeded in reconciling him somewhat to his disappointment. After a few months his family arrived, and they are now happily situated on a good farm in San José Valley.

My friend Brown, from Baltimore, had two disappointments before his wife arrived. At the time he expected her he boarded the steamer, and learned to his sorrow that she was not aboard. He then thought the next steamer would bring her without a doubt, and at most he would have to wait only two weeks.

Those were long, dreary weeks, but he was a good

fellow, and waited patiently; and when the steamer got in he was on hand in good time, you may be sure. Rushing aboard he inquired:

"Is Mrs. Brown aboard? is Mrs. Brown aboard?"

"O yes," replied one who seemed to know; "she is in her state-room, No. —."

He hastily took the circuit of the state-rooms to find the number. Mrs. Brown heard in the mean time that her beloved husband was aboard, and was filled with ecstasies. Finally Brown found her state-room, and sprang in to embrace his wife, when O! shocking to their hopes! they found it was neither of them; he was not the man, and she was not the woman!

Soon after, however, his wife and family arrived, and they are living happily together, and are exemplary members of the Methodist Episcopal Church in California.

I had another Baltimore friend, who was a widower. Having at home two very interesting daughters, and a second wife engaged, he sent for the three to come together to California. He put on his extras and went to greet his daughters and intended bride, but was met by his youngest daughter, who alone was left to tell the sad tale that the other two had suddenly sickened and died, and found a grave in the coral depths of the Pacific. That was a dark day for poor Wm. H. Middleton. Another friend of mine had his family coming out in that splendid clipper ship, the "Queen of the Seas." When she was due, I was told that he prepared a great feast, and invited about two hundred guests to celebrate the occasion of his wife's arrival. When he boarded the ship his little daughter met him, and pointed him to a box which lay in a boat on the hurricane deck, securely folded in tarpaulin, and said to him, "There's mother!" She had been a corpse for three months.

But notwithstanding the distance and dangers, and extraordinary difficulties attending emigration to California, and the numerous deaths and disappointments recorded and not recorded, the yearly caravans across the plains, and the semi-monthly arrivals in San Francisco, have sufficed already to dot the great social Sahara of California with more than ten thousand oases. By the introduction of good families, and the socializing and purifying institutions of the Gospel, living waters have broken "out in the wilderness, and streams in the desert."

CHAPTER VIII.

HOSPITAL REMINISCENCES IN SAN FRANCISCO.

In the fall of 1849, as I walked down Clay-street, one day, my eye rested on a sign, in large red letters, "CITY HOSPITAL." I stopped and gazed at it till my soul was thrilled with horror. The letters looked as if they were written with blood, and I said to myself, Ah! that's the depot of death, where the fast adventurers of California, young men in manhood's strength, stricken down by the hand of disease, are cast out of the train and left to perish. There all their bright hopes and visions of future wealth and weal expire, and are buried forever. There are husbands, and sons, and brothers, thousands of miles from sympathizing kindred and friends, dying in destitution and despair. Shall I not be a brother to the sick stranger in California, and tell him of that heavenly Friend "that sticketh closer than a brother?" The cross of intruding myself into strange hospitals, and offering my services to the promiscuous masses of the sick and dying of all nations and creeds, was, to my unobtrusive nature, very heavy, but I there resolved to take it up, a decision which I have never regretted. I went immediately to the said hospital and inquired for the physician who had it in charge; introduced myself to him, and told him the object of my call, to which he replied: "I can readily appreciate your motives, but then you must know, sir, that we have very sick men in every room, who could not bear any noise. Anything like singing or praying might greatly excite them and make them worse. I would prefer that you would not visit the wards unless some particular man wishes to see you."

"Well, doctor," I replied, "I certainly would not wish to do anything that would be injurious to any patient, but I have been accustomed to visit the sick, and think I so understand my business as to talk, and sing, and pray, or do whatever may seem appropriate, not only without injury to any one, but in a manner that will even contribute to the improvement of their physical condition. By diverting their minds from the dark realities of their own condition and unhappy surroundings, and by interesting them in some new associations and themes of thought, I may impart to their minds vigor and hope, and mind, and heart, and will may unite with gathering strength, and make successful resistance against disease. Those who are hopelessly diseased cannot receive much injury from my visits, while I may be instrumental in benefiting their departing souls. If you please, doctor," I continued, "you can go with me, or send a man to point out the men to whom you do not wish me to speak, and to see that I do no injury to any one."

Said the doctor: "I have no time to go with you, and nobody to send."

Another doctor present then added: "It is not proper that he should go through the hospital."

At that moment an old man, who had been sitting in the office listening to our conversation, said:

"Doctor, there are many sick men in the hospital, who, I know, would be very glad to receive a visit from this gentleman; and if you will allow me, sir, I will conduct him through the rooms."

The doctor replied: "Very well. Take him up stairs first, and then down to the lower wards."

"Ay, ay, sir," said the old tar, as he beckoned me after him up the stairs. He introduced me to every patient in the house, and made a greater ado over my arrival at the hospital than if the *alcalde* had visited them. I was first conducted through the "pay rooms;" the departments of those who, in whole or in part, paid for their keeping. Many small rooms had but from two to four men in them. Others, larger, had as many as twelve. I spoke to each patient, inquiring after their condition of health, and the state of their souls. I then addressed a few words of sympathy and religious instruction to all in the room collectively, sung a few verses in a soft strain, and prayed in an audible, but subdued tone, adapting the petition, as near as possible, to the wants of their individual cases as I had learned them; and so passed on, performing similar services in each room. Darius Carter, of Baltimore, who gave me fifty dollars for my California chapel, also gave me ten dollars' worth of tracts, which I distributed principally in the hospital, to the great comfort of many who had nothing else to read, and nothing to do but read. The patients at first seemed very inquisitive to know my object in visiting them, and many at first refused to take tracts, saying, "I have no money;" but when they learned from myself and my earnest old captain, that my visit was gratuitous, and my tracts the same, they expressed great surprise and gratitude. Some of them said that they had never supposed that anybody in California ever thought of doing anything but for money.

After going through the pay rooms, I was next conducted across a yard to a separate one-story building, about thirty by forty feet in size, divided into two wards, each containing from forty to fifty sick men. Here the city patients, proper, were confined together as closely as possible, and allow room between their cots for one person to pass. I thought the up-stair rooms were filthy enough to kill any well man, who would there confine himself for a short period; but I now saw that, in comparison with the others, they were entitled to be called *choice* rooms, for the privilege of dying in which a man who had money might well afford to pay high rates. But these "lower wards" were so offensive to the eye, and especially to the olfactories, that it was with great difficulty I could remain long enough to do the singing, praying, and talking I deemed my duty.

The ordinary comforts, and even the necessaries of life in California, in those days, were very rare and costly; and to the patients were things to be remembered in the experience of the past, only to add, by contrast, a keener edge to their present sorrows.

The nurses were generally men, devoid of sympathy, careless, rude in their care of the sick, and exceedingly vulgar and profane. One hundred dollars per month was about as low as anything in the shape of a man could be hired, and hence hospital nurses were not only the most worthless of men, but insufficient in number to attend adequately to their duties.

I remember a poor fellow, by the name of Switzer, died in one of these wards, who told me that he lay whole nights suffering, in addition to the pains of mortal disease, the ragings of thirst, without a drop of water to wet his lips. A cup of tea was set in the evening upon a shelf over his head, but his strength was gone, and he had no more power to reach it than a man on a gibbet. He was a Christian, too, a member of the Congregational Church, and I have no doubt went from there to heaven. When he got to that country in which "there is no more death, neither sorrow nor crying," and looked back to the place where he left his corruptible body, the contrast must have filled him with unutterable surprise.

The most prevalent and fatal disease in California at that time was chronic diarrhea and dysentery, a consumption of the bowels, very similar, in its debilitating mortal effect upon the constitution, to consumption of the lungs. Men afflicted with this disease have been seen moping about the streets, looking like the personification of death and despair, for weeks, till strength, and money, and friends were gone, and then, as a last resort, they were carried to the hospital, to pass a few miserable weeks more in one of those filthy wards, where they often died, I was told by the patients, in the night, without any one knowing the time of their departure. In the morning, when the nurses passed round, they found and reported the dead. A plain coffin was immediately brought, for a supply was kept on hand, and laid beside the cot of the deceased, and he was lifted from the cot just as he died, laid in the coffin, and carried out to the dead cart, the driver of which was seen daily plodding through the mud to the graveyard, near North Beach, with from one to three corpses at a load.

While many lingered on the confines of death for weeks, I have often seen men enter those horrible wards with apparently very slight indisposition, and within a few days wilt down and die. I wondered that *any* could survive in such a place for a longer period. The city was then paying for the care of those patients five dollars per day, an amount, one would think, sufficient to furnish a motive, if not to cure and discharge the patients, at least to prolong their lives as long as possible; but I suppose they made as profitable a speculation out of the multiplication of new cases as they could do by protracting the lives of the old ones; and hence, no matter how fast they died, others took their places, who for a time, perhaps, required less attention.

It turned out that the old man who piloted me through the hospital on my first visit was an old ship master, Captain A. Welch. He introduced me that day to his friend Captain Lock, who died soon after, having after my visit professed to find peace through Jesus, and a preparation for heaven. Captain Welch told me that seeing his friend neglected, he said to the doctor: "Captain Lock has had no attention for forty-eight hours, and is dying from sheer neglect."

"Well," replied the doctor, "let him die, the sooner the better. The world can well spare him, and the community will be relieved when he is gone." He died that night. Before his death he gave his clothing to his friend Captain Welch, but the captain told him he would not touch a thing he had while he was alive, but as soon as he was gone the nurse relieved the captain of any trouble with the effects of the deceased man.

The doctor fell out with Captain Welch, because he spoke his mind so freely, and threatened to turn him out of the hospital.

"Yes," said Captain Welch, in reply, "I saw Captain —— pay you for the ten days he had been in here eighty-six dollars, and after his death you collected the same bill from his friends. Now, sir, if you want me to show you up, just turn me out."

The doctor then took his cot from him, and the captain said: "Doctor, where shall I sleep, sir?"

"Sleep there on the floor," replied the doctor, pointing to a corner where they laid out the dead, when it was too late in the evening, or the weather too bad, to remove them directly from their cot of death to the dead cart.

The captain said he lay there one night with four corpses around him, and could hardly get his breath. I have heard patients complain of very foul play toward those who had money, but sick men are apt to be sensitive and suspicious, especially in such a place as that, and I always hoped those things were not so bad as represented; but from what I saw I had my fears for the safety of any man's life who had money, in the hospital at the time of which I speak.

The hospital changed hands several times, however, within a few months, and one or two good physicians, and I believe honest and kind-hearted men, had for a short time the care of the sick, and were really working a reform in the old hospital, before the whole care of the city patients was, in 1850, transferred to Doctor Peter Smith, in a new hospital, near the corner of Clay and Powell streets, where the sick had better accommodations, and more attention shown them.

Old Captain Welch was in the old hospital over a year, and would doubtless have died if he had been confined to his room, but he was out where he could get pure air most of his time. He had a very sore leg, and the doctor told him that it was mortifying and would have to be amputated. Finally several doctors came into his room with a table, and a lot of surgical instrument, and said to him, "Come, captain, we want to lash you to this table, and take off that bad leg of yours."

"I won't have my leg taken off," replied the captain.

"If you don't," said the doctor, "you are a dead man, or as good as dead, for that leg is mortified now."

"Well," said the captain, "if I die I'll die with both legs on me."

The doctor became enraged, and said to him: "If you don't obey orders immediately, and submit to the rules of this house, you shall leave it this day."

"Very well," rejoined the captain. "And that very day," said the captain to me since, "I took up my sore leg and walked off with it, and have not been back since." He is the same Captain Welch who since received a medal from some New-York citizens for his success in rescuing a number of the poor survivors of the wrecked "steamer San Francisco," and is now employed as colporteur and Bible distributer in the city of New-York.

John Purseglove, a good Methodist brother, who had just arrived in the city, sick and destitute, was sent to the hospital; but finding that he was sinking daily, and would soon die if he remained there, he prayed to the Lord to give him strength to get off his bed and walk away. He said he believed the Lord would help him, and according to his faith so was his effort, for he immediately crawled out, and without saying a word to doctor, or nurse, or anybody, he scrambled away by the aid of a couple of sticks, determined, if he must die, to die somewhere else. Some of the brethren soon found him, and fitted up a room for him and supplied his wants till he recovered. He believes to this day, that by leaving the hospital he slipped right out of the clutches of death.

Sick and destitute members of our Church have generally been cared for by the brethren in San Francisco. I have no recollection of more than three Methodists who died in the San Francisco hospital, and they were sick on their arrival, and had never been reported to the Church. Indeed there were but very few hospital patients connected with any Church. I met with many backsliders there who had once been Church members, but were not then.

An extraordinary degree of liberality has always been shown by the masses of Californians toward the sick and destitute. But few men, it is true, would give their *time* even to carry a dying man out of the streets, but would freely give their money on application. Then again, the Order of Free and Accepted Masons, who organized a Lodge in San Francisco as early as October, 1849, and now number five or six thousand members in the state, have done a vast amount of work, and expended several hundred thousand dollars for the relief of the suffering and destitute in California. The Indepedent Order of Odd Fellows, who organized about the same time, have fully measured up with the Masons, according to my best information, in numbers, charitable works, and liberality.

Other charitable institutions have each done their part, and the Churches of various denominations have displayed great liberality, not only for the relief of their own destitute members, but in response to the calls of the suffering of every variety. A vast amount of money has been raised to pay the homeward passage of destitute maimed and sick men. I remember a case, for illustration, of a man by the name of Peter Deal, who in the summer of 1851 came one night to a love-feast in our church on Powell-street, and told a good story about his religious enjoyments, his afflictions, destitution, desire to go home to his family, etc. None of us had ever seen him before; but at the close of the meeting the brethren raised for him one hundred and forty dollars to pay his passage home. Similar calls for passage-money were made, as regularly as the sailing of the steamers, on the Churches generally, and the people at large, and wherever a hope of success presented itself. Many hundred dollars have been contributed by the crowds attending preaching on the Plaza to assist poor fellows who, by sickness or otherwise, were disabled, to get back to their families and friends.

To transcribe in detail the hospital scenes which have been daguerreotyped on the tablets of my memory during a period of seven years in San Francisco, would make a volume so large, and so revolting to humanity in its delineations, that the reader would sicken and turn away from it before he could read half through it. Our purpose, therefore, in these reminiscences, is simply to present a few specimen scenes, and individual cases of hope and of despair occurring at different periods in the history of that city. As a general description, I would remark, the City Hospital of San Francisco, from 1849 up to the present, has always had a great variety of patients, ranging in number from one hundred to three hundred and fifty. The largest number of the patients were Americans, and foreigners who spoke the English language. The next in number were Frenchmen, and then Germans, and Spaniards, and Scandinavians, Russians, Portuguese, Italians, Turks, Islanders of various tribes, Chinamen, etc.

My usual mode of visitation was to speak personally to as many as possible; inquire into their condition and wants, bodily, spiritual, and otherwise; act as amanuensis for the sick and dying, recording last messages to friends at home; get letters out of the post-office, and convey them to the sick; carry messages to friends in the city; and in very early days, when waiters were scarce, I often ministered to the bodily wants of the sick, dressed blisters, turned or raised patients, fixed their beds, gave them drink, and sometimes comforted the convalescing with a little of Mrs. Taylor's good home-made bread, and gave them such advice as I thought might be useful to them.

In the winter of 1849–50, we had a great many scurvy patients in the hospital; many of whom had been on long voyages, living for months on what the sailors call "old junk" and ship-bread; all the fresh meat they got was found in a live state in their bread. Poor fellows! they had come to a bad market, where potatoes were fifty cents per pound, and scarcely any other vegetables to be had at any price. There they were, confined in the bad atmosphere of the hospital, swallowing drugs and dry provisions, sinking down and dying daily. One day, as I entered a large ward filled with such patients, I looked at them and thought a minute on their wretched condition, and then I said, "My friends, what are you doing here? You are cooped up in this miserable place, without fresh air, without sunshine, without exercise, and without vegetable diet. You will die, the last man of you, if you don't get out of this place. You had better be turned out in San José Valley to graze, like old Nebuchadnezzar, than pine away and die in such a place as this. Now," said I, "I'll tell you what will cure you. On those sand-hills back of the city there grows a kind of wild lettuce," which I described to them. "If you will go out and gather that lettuce and use it, with a little vinegar, it will cure you. I knew the open air, and sunshine, and exercise would help them, and believed the prescribed salad the best thing for them within their reach. It was an interesting sight to see those poor fellows under the inspiration of a new hope, crawling out and scrambling up the hills in search of my prescribed cure. The next week, when I called again to see them, I was really surprised to see how much their condition had improved. When I entered, some of the poor fellows wept, and others laughed, and after a grateful greeting they said: "You've saved our lives, sir; your prescription has done us more good than all the medicines and all the doctors in the city could do for us." The most of them soon afterward recovered and left the hospital. As a spiritual adviser in my hospital visits, I generally addressed them personally, and tried to lead them to seek an acquaintance with the sinner's Friend. I then usually sung in each ward, in a soft tone, one, two, or three appropriate pieces, and prayed for them collectively and personally, so far as I had been able to learn their personal condition and wants, and frequently, either before or after prayer, made some remarks in the form of an exhortation to be reconciled to God. I usually introduced religious exercises by saying: "If my brethren in affliction have no objections, we will sing a few verses and have a word of prayer together." I do not remember of ever hearing an objection made but once, and that was by a poor man who became very much ashamed of his conduct before the exercises were over. Many, to be sure, seemed careless and indifferent, read novels while I prayed, and never seemed to profit by what I said, but a large majority seemed to appreciate very highly my efforts for their good. Even foreigners, who could not understand my language, seemed greatly interested, especially in my singing.

I was once traveling in San José Valley, and passing in sight of a company of Spaniards, who had stopped at a spring of water to refresh themselves, one of them came running to me, and grasped my hand as though I had been a brother he had not seen for a dozen years. For a moment I could not tell how to interpret his conduct; but I immediately recognized him as a man I had often seen in the hospital. He had been a great sufferer, and I had many times bent over him and inquired after his welfare, and it seemed that my attentions to him, or the singing, or something else, had made a deep impression on him.

I think, however, from all I could see and learn, that not more than an average of one hospital patient in thirty was a professor of experimental religion. About an average of one in every five showed signs of penitence; but of those not more than one in twenty made a profession of religion.

In my book on "Street Preaching" there is a chapter of "triumphant death scenes," in which is given a number of cases of hopeful conversion to God among hospital patients; but those, alas! are but the exceptions, and not the rule. The rule is for men to die as they have lived.

The question is often asked in regard to a departed friend: "How did he die? Was he prepared?" A more appropriate inquiry is: "How did he live?" "Tell me how he lived, and I'll tell you how he died," unless he is one of the rare exceptions referred to. I, however, never feel like giving a sinner up this side the gates of perdition, for we are not saved by works of righteousness which we have done, but by the mercy of God through the merits of Jesus; and if a man, even in the grasp of death, can fully submit to the will of God, and "believe in the Lord Jesus Christ," I know of nothing to prevent his being saved from sin, and washed in the blood of sprinkling, and thus prepared for heaven.

But the difficulty which I have seen illustrated in the experience of thousands of sick and dying men, consists in the fact that the principles and habits which have been developed and matured by a life of rebellion against God, are, according to the constitutional laws of mind, still strong and controlling in death, and the stronger, frequently, because of the enfeebled, distracted condition of the soul amid the wreck of its tabernacle.

The dreadful habit of procrastination, for example, is about as common and all-conquering in sickness and death as it is in life and health.

I remember, after pleading with a dying man to give his heart to God, he said: "O, it's not worth while now; I'm getting better; I'll soon be well. I feel no pain at all, and nothing ails me now but want of breath. I can't breathe easy; but I'll soon be relieved of that."

Poor man! I could then hear distinctly the death-rattle in his throat, and yet he would not believe that there was any danger. In a few hours he was a corpse.

I remember a fine-looking young man from New-York, whom I tried hard to lead to Christ; and after talking, and singing, and praying with him, and doing everything I could to induce him to try and seek Jesus, I said to him: "Now, my dear brother, when will you begin to pray, and try to give your heart to God?"

"Well," said he, "I think I will make a commencement in about three weeks."

The poor fellow, though he would not believe it, was dying then, and I knew it, and hence continued to press the subject of a preparation on his attention till he drew the cover over his head to escape my appeals. A few hours afterward he was covered with the pall of death.

Young C. M. was accidentally shot, and immediately sent for me in such haste that the messenger stopped me in the midst of a street sermon, and entreated me to go at once and try to relieve the mind of the dying man. When I presented myself beside his bloody bed, he said:

"Father Taylor, I'm glad you've come; but O! I'm in such pain I can't talk, nor pray, nor do anything now. Please call again in an hour; perhaps by that time I'll feel better."

I prayed with him, and called again at the appointed time, and found him gasping in his last struggle.

Without noting a hundred such cases, as I might, which have come under my own observation, I will, for the further illustration of the subject, add but one other case.

He was a very genteel-looking man, who died with cholera in the hospital during the fall of 1850. He was in a collapsed state when I found him. I said to him: "My dear brother, have you made your peace with God?"

"No, sir," answered he; "I can't say that I have."

"Do you not pray to the Lord sometimes to have mercy on you, and for the sake of Jesus to pardon your sins?"

"No, sir."

"Have you never prayed?"

"No, sir, never in my life."

"You believe in the Divine reality of religion, and that we may have our sins all forgiven, and enjoy the conscious evidence of pardon, do you not?"

"Yes, sir, I believe in religion, and think it a very good thing to have."

He was calm and composed; his dreadful paroxysms had passed, and the fatal work was done. He was then poised on an eddying wave of death's dark tide, which on its next swell would whirl him out of the bounds of time into the breakers of eternal seas beyond. I saw his peril, and pulled with all my might to bring the life-boat of mercy by his side. I got very near to him, and entreated him to try to get into it and save his soul, but I could not prevail on him to make an effort; under the force of the ruling habit of his life he coolly said:

"Well, I'll think about it."

How true the sentiment of an English bard:

> "Procrastination is the thief of time;
> Year after year it steals till all is gone,
> And to the mercy of a moment leaves
> The vast concerns of an eternal state."

But horrible to relate, that last moment on which hangs the soul's eternal destiny, is hooked by the same insidious rogue, and then and forever all is lost!

Next to the horrible habit of procrastination, and closely allied with it, is that of indifference and moral insensibility, that dreadful state thus described by St. Paul: "Having the understanding darkened, being alienated from the life of God through the ignorance that is in them, because of the blindness of their heart: who being past feeling have given themselves over unto lasciviousness, to work all uncleanness with greediness." This state of mind in some cases manifests itself in reckless self-deception, and in many more in the blindest stupidity and indifference in regard to the future of their souls.

A dying sailor, originally from Buffalo, N. Y., whom I exhorted to be reconciled to God, said:

"I don't think it makes much difference whether I have religion or not. I have always lived a straightforward, upright life, like other sailors, and I can't see what more is required."

A very good-looking young man said, in reply to my entreaties on behalf of his soul:

"I have not prayed, and don't intend to. God Almighty can do with me what he likes; I shan't concern myself about it."

He then turned over, shut his eyes to sleep, and woke up in eternity.

When to this soul-destroying habit of indifference there is added a surfeit of drugs and opiates, there is but little more power of thought, feeling, prayer, or repentance than might be expected of the dead. I have seen hundreds of poor fellows sleeping away their lives without any apparent consciousness of danger; and I have heard men call this peaceful dying!

J. M'. died of cholera at a boarding-house kept by a Scotchman, who sent for me to attend his funeral, and said to me on the occasion, in regard to the deceased: "He was a good man. One of the best men I ever had in my house, and he died in great peace. He did not speak a word for twenty-four hours before his death. Ah! he was a good man; to be sure, he would take a glass of grog now and then, and was fond of a game of cards, and sometimes would swear a little, but he didn't mean any harm by that, for he was a good man, and died in great peace."

A great many, however, of those whom I have seen in the death struggle, shook off the apathy I have described, and awoke to the keenest sensibilities of conscience, and the most dreadful forebodings of future ill; but a large majority of such wrapped themselves closely in the mantle of despair, so dark and impervious that no ray of hope could reach their souls. A dying young man from Michigan said, in an agony of emotion: "O that I had sought religion when I might! but I put it off, and now I'm so weak in body and mind it is no use to try. Too late now!"

A gentleman from Boston, very near his end, said to me:

"My friends are nearly all religious; I have passed through a great many revivals, and have had a great many pressing invitations and opportunities to seek religion. How easy it would then have been for me to have given my heart to God. What a fool I was. Why did I not embrace religion and be a happy man? I should then have been ready for this hour. But alas! I did not when I might, and now I cannot."

A poor young man said as he was nearing the grave: "When I try to pray my mind becomes deranged, and I'm so weak I cannot pray."

When Mr. R., from Baltimore, was seized with cholera, he sent for me to come and see him, and said to me, when I entered his room: "My wife, who is a Christian woman, has been writing me ever since I came here to make your acquaintance, and attend your church, but I have not done it; and what is worse, I am about to leave the world without a preparation to meet God." He was as noble-looking a man as could be found in a thousand, and knowing many of his friends in Baltimore I felt the greatest possible sympathy for him; my soul loved him, and I determined, if possible, to contest the devil's claim on him to the last moment of his life. But he was in despair, and after laboring with him about an hour, in urging him to try to fix his mind on some precious promise of the Bible, he said:

"There is but one passage in the Bible that I can call to mind, and that haunts me. I can think of nothing else, for it exactly suits my case: 'He that being often reproved hardeneth his heart, shall suddenly be destroyed, and that without remedy.' Mr. Taylor," continued he, "it's no use to talk to me, or to try to do anything further; I am that man, and my doom is fixed."

The next day when I entered his room he said to a couple of young men present, "Go out, boys; I want to talk to Mr. Taylor." Then he said: "I have no hope, my doom is fixed; but, for the warning of others, I want to tell you something that occurred a few months ago. I was then in health, and doing a good business, and a man said to me, 'Dick, how would you like to have a clerkship?' and I replied, 'I wouldn't have a clerkship under Jesus Christ.' Now, sir, that is the way I treated Christ when I thought I did not need him; and now when I'm dying, and can do no better for this life, it's presumption to offer myself to him. It is no use; he won't have me."

Nothing that I could say seemed to have any effect toward changing his mind. A few hours afterward, when he felt the icy grasp of death upon his heart, he cried, "Boys, help me out of this place!"

"O no, Dick, you're too sick; we cannot help you up."

"O do help me up; I can't lie here."

"O Dick, don't exert yourself so: you'll hasten your death."

"Boys," said the poor fellow, "if you don't help me up, I'll cry Murder!" and with that he cried at the top of his voice, which was yet strong and clear, "Murder! murder! murder!" till life's tide ebbed out, and his voice was hushed in death. How dreadful the hazard of postponing the business of life, the great object for which life is given, to the hour when heart and flesh are failing!

The City Hospital has changed hands many times, and its location has been changed nearly as often as its resident physicians. It has also changed its name, bearing for several years past the title of "State Marine Hospital." No permanent improvements for the comfort of city patients have been made. The city has always borne the enormous tax of heavy rents for hospital accommodations, with all other inconveniences of renters.

There have been several private hospitals in the city, Dr. Stout's and Dr. Shuler's being the most largely patronized; and the French citizens have built one, that will accommodate perhaps one hundred patients, on some kind of a joint stock principle, by which each subscriber is entitled to its privileges.

But the only permanent public building of this kind in the city is the UNITED STATES MARINE HOSPITAL. It is located on Rincon Point, on an elevation affording a grand view of the city and bay of San Francisco, the Contra Costa valleys and hills, and the coast range mountains. The city authorities conveyed to the United States six fifty vara lots, each one hundred and thirty-seven and a half feet square, as a site for the institution, and it was built by United States authority at a cost of two hundred and twenty thousand dollars, appropriated from a fund created by a tax on all American sailors, of twenty-five cents per month, which shipmasters are required to deduct from their wages, and pay at the custom-house.

In return for this tax every sailor belonging to American vessels is entitled, in case of illness, to a certificate from the collector of the port, for admission into the hospital which has been built, and is furnished and supported by his money, so that he enters not as a charity patient, but as one of the owners of the institution. The United States Marine Hospital in San Francisco will accommodate comfortably about five hundred patients, and is kept in the most perfect order; the floors, furniture, and everything almost as neat and clean as a new dollar.

There is no regular chaplain in this hospital, but I introduced regular religious services there on Sab-

UNITED STATES MARINE HOSPITAL.

bath soon after it was built, which I kept up during most of my subsequent stay in California; and which are still kept up by local preachers, exhorters, and occasional visits from regular pastors.

My first preaching appointment there is thus noted in my journal:

"*Monday, December* 26, 1853.—When at the United States Marine Hospital last week, I made an arrangement with Dr. M'Millen, the resident physician, to have preaching there at nine o'clock every Sunday morning. The doctor was very cordial in his affirmative response to my proposition, and gave me choice of any room in the house. The dining-room being a very popular room with the convalescing sailors, convenient, easy of access, very clean, and well provided with seats, I selected that as the preaching-place, where the bread of life should be dispensed to hungry souls without money and without price. I accordingly went up yesterday morning, and found my chapel, the dining-room, in order, and at the ringing of the breakfast-bell the congregation assembled. At this time there are but about seventy patients there, and many of them are unable to leave their rooms; but we had an audience of thirty-five men of the sea, who listened with great attention, and many of them with tears, to a discourse from: 'O wretched man that I am! who shall deliver me from the body of this death?' There was evidently a gracious influence felt by all on the occasion, and I am much pleased with the prospect of good at that appointment, by the Lord's help."

Those who were unable to attend preaching I visited in their wards, and sung, and prayed, and talked to them; but my ward visits were generally during the week. I had been preaching very frequently in the City Hospital for several years prior to the opening of the United States Marine Hospital; but subsequently, while I continued my visits to the former through the week, I continued to preach only in the latter. A carpenter, by the name of J. H. Perry, employed as one of the hands in the erection of this magnificent building, embraced religion while at work up in the fourth story, and joined our Bethel Society, and became a very consistent Christian. If my space permitted it I might here record many incidents, and some hopeful conversions, among seamen, coming under my observation in connection with my visits to this noble institution.

CHAPTER IX.

EXTENT AND RESOURCES OF CALIFORNIA.

When I set sail for California in the spring of 1849, the prevailing idea among the people generally seemed to be, that California was a small peninsula on the Pacific coast, a place of but little importance, except for the gold diggings which had been discovered there, which would be worked out in a few years, and then the country would be abandoned to the Indians and wolves; that everybody lived in San Francisco, and worked in the mines near by. I carried a large package of letters round Cape Horn, the writers of them believing that though the conveyance did not belong to the *fast* line, it was, nevertheless, the most reliable, as I would be certain to meet all their California friends on my arrival in San Francisco.

The emigration of 1849, though they found California an astonishingly large country, yet arriving there in the dry season, they regarded the entire territory, except a few irrigated garden spots, as a vast barren desert. But few persons, even after a sojourn of two years there, could believe that California soil would produce grain or vegetables without irrigation. But few had faith enough to put the question to a practical test, and it was not until a few hopeful, adventurous farmers, who were willing to hazard their money and their reputation for soundness of mind, had made a fortune out of the products of their unirrigated fields, that the mass of the people were gradually led to change their views.

The potato-growing fever then set in, and raged like the gold mania. Hundreds of thousands of dollars were invested in the potato-crop. Fifteen cents per pound were paid for seed potatoes, and one hundred dollars per month paid each man to fence and prepare the land and attend to the crop. The result was that the markets were glutted, the price of potatoes went down to the cost value of the sacks that contained them, and hundreds of thousands of tons of the finest potatoes in the world, dug and gathered into large cribs, lay and rotted, creating such a nuisance that it was feared that they would breed a pestilence in some localities. A friend of mine offered a man his crop if he would take them away. "O," replied the man, "I can do better than that; I can get them on the same terms nearer home, and save the freight." Another friend of mine lost fifty thousand dollars on a single crop. Some poor fellows paid very dear for the experience, but it convinced the people that the great California desert was more productive than any fruitful land they had ever seen. No Californian now doubts that the agricultural resources of the country are immense beyond adequate computation, but I find masses of persons on the Atlantic side who have very limited views of California, both in regard to the extent of her domain, and her exhaustless resources. Many persons, whose views are based on a mere glance at statistical exhibits, remind me of a school-boy in Lexington, Virginia. He was regarded as a great proficient in the study of geography; always "stood head in his class." During vacation he made a visit to Staunton, a distance of thirty-five miles, to see his aunt. On his return his associates hailed him: "Halloo, John! how did you like your visit to Staunton?" "O, I was perfectly delighted! I had no idea that the world was so big."

That portion of the little peninsula we used to trace, in school-boy days, on the map of the Pacific coast, and spell out its hard name, "Californy," embraced in the State of California, extends along the coast from 32° 40′ 13″ to 41° 44′ 41″, north latitude, embracing a coast line, from San Diego to Crescent City, of about seven hundred miles, with an average width back to the Sierra Nevada Mountains, of about two hundred miles.

The total area of the state, including lakes, bays, and precipitous mountains, is carefully estimated at ninty-nine millions, four hundred and sixty-three thousand, six hundred and eighty acres. To form a comparative idea of the extent of such a patch of land, take the states of Maine, Vermont, New-Hampshire, Massachusetts, Connecticut, Rhode Island, New-York, Pennsylvania, New-Jersey, Delaware, and Maryland, and spread them all out together on the broad bosom of California, and they will leave an uncovered margin of thirteen thousand seven hundred and seventy-four square miles. This surplus margin might be divided up into ten such states as Rhode Island, and still you would have one hundred and seventy-four square miles left, which you might appropriate for "Indian reservations."

The amount of land in the State of California, adapted to the purposes of agriculture is estimated at forty-one millions, six hundred and twenty-two thousand, and four hundred acres, exclusive of the swamp and overflowed lands, estimated at five millions, which, when reclaimed, will produce every variety of crops. The amount of grazing land is estimated at thirty millions of acres, making a total of seventy-six millions, six hundred and twenty-two thousand acres of land, suitable for agricultural and stock-raising purposes. The amount of land inclosed for agricultural purposes is about six hundred and twenty-eight thousand acres.

The area of gold mining land is variously estimated at from eleven to fifteen millions of acres; suppose we say in definite numbers twelve millions; which, added to the agricultural and grazing portions just named, would make an aggregate of eighty-eight millions, six hundred and twenty-two thousand four hundred acres of productive land in the State of California, leaving ten millions eight hundred and forty-one thousand two hundred and eighty acres, for the accommodation of grizzly bears and California lions.

"In the year 1856 there were 578,963 acres in California cultivated in cereal grain. Wheat, 176,963 acres, yielding 3,979,032 bushels. Barley, 154,674 acres, yielding 4,639,678 bushels. Oats, 37,602 acres, yielding 1,263,359 bushels. The average yield of wheat in 1856 was twenty-three bushels per acre, which, owing to the severe drought of the early part of the season, was much less than that of previous years. The ordinary average is about thirty bushels per acre, taking the crop of the entire state together. The average yield of barley is thirty bushels per acre. It frequently yields from fifty to seventy-five bushels per acre. The average yield of the oat crop is thirty-three bushels per acre. Crops of this grain have frequently averaged seventy-five bushels per acre; and a crop of thirty-two acres in Alameda County, which received a premium at the State Agricultural fair for 1856, averaged one hundred and thirty-four bushels to the acre."

One peculiarity in California grain growing is, that two or three crops are generally raised from one sowing. After the first crop is harvested, and the field gleaned by the hogs, it is then closed up, generally without a replowing, or anything, till the next harvest-time, when a better crop is sometimes gathered than the first. In case of severe drought the second crop is the most reliable, from the fact that it takes root with the first fall rains before seeding-time commences, and comes earlier to the harvest.

The visiting committee of the California Agricultural Society, in their report for the year 1856, have the following notice of a field of barley: "Near Alviso, Santa Clara County, there is a field of barley, fifty acres in extent, which has averaged the present season forty-three bushels to the acre. This is the fifth crop from a single sowing; it has received no special care, and may be regarded as a memorable example of a succession of volunteer crops." Two crops are almost invariably expected from one sowing; the third is not generally relied on.

"The returns from thirty-four counties of the state exhibit the crop of Indian corn, of 1856, at 11,020 acres, averaging for the entire crop thirty one bushels per acre. Rye averages about thirty bushels per acre. Buckwheat about twenty-five bushels per acre. Beans average about thirty bushels per acre, and peas twenty-eight. The number of acres planted in potatoes in the year 1856, are sixteen thousand four hundred and thirty-four, averaging, in Alameda County, seventy bushels; Sacramento, one hundred; San Joaquin, two hundred; Siskiyou, one hundred; and Trinity, three hundred bushels per acre.

"The returns of twenty-two counties exhibit fourteen thousand seven hundred and three acres planted with vegetables. It is probable that the remaining counties will increase this amount to about forty-five thousand acres."

Some rare specimens of vegetables and fruit were exhibited at the State Agricultural Fair of 1856. I saw them myself, and have no doubt as to the correctness of the published statements in regard to them. There were exhibited "two pumpkins from Sacramento, weighing two hundred and ten, and two hundred and forty pounds." Those were "*some punkins*," were they not?

A beet, grown by Colonel Hall, of Sacramento City, weighing seventy-three pounds; a carrot, weighing ten pounds, measuring one foot and eight inches in circumference, and three feet and three inches in length. There were fifty in the same bed of equal size. The seeds were sown on June 25th, and the carrots dug September 20th. A tomato, seventeen inches in circumference; a squash, weighing one hundred and forty-one pounds; an onion, weighing two pounds and fifteen ounces, and measuring twenty inches in circumference; a cornstalk, twenty-one feet and nine inches in height; watermelons, from near Nevada, twenty-seven gave an aggregate of five hundred and fifty pounds; a sweet potato, from San José, weighing eleven pounds and two ounces; an Irish potato, from Bodega, weighing seven and a quarter pounds; a bunch of potatoes, of the Oregon red variety, from a single eye, weighing ten pounds."

I would here remark that in California the best potatoes are selected for seed, cut up carefully, and but one eye put in a hill.

"Grapes, several bunches, weighing over four pounds each; a citron lemon, sixteen and a half by eighteen and three quarter inches in circumference, weighing two pounds and fourteen ounces, from Los Angeles; fig-tree, a slip one foot in length, and five eighths of an inch in thickness, was planted April 1st, and in the month of September following was eleven feet and six inches high, and nine and a quarter inches in circumference at the base, with a corresponding growth of branches; peach-trees, in twenty-eight months from the planting of the seed, bore fruit over nine inches in circumference, and weighing from seven to eight and a half ounces; there were thirty-four of these large peaches on one tree; an apple, measuring fifteen and one third inches in circumference each way, weighing twenty-three ounces, grown in the Yamhill Orchard."

Those large apples are called "Gloria Mundi." Soon after their first appearance in the San Francisco markets I bought one of them for three dollars. I felt a little conscience-stricken for paying that much for one apple; but Mrs. Taylor was in very delicate health at that time, and a little discouraged, so I thought that the sight of such a specimen of the "fruits of the land" would do her more good, and be cheaper than a doctor's prescription. I believed we would get at least three dollars' worth of hope out of it, and then the apple itself would be clear gain, which would not be, upon the whole, a bad speculation.

Brother Owen and I were looking at some of those great apples one day, and the price seemed to take Owen aback. After expressing his surprise, said he to the fruit-vender:

"How much will you charge me for the privilege of smelling one of them?"

"Nothing at all, sir," replied the fruit man.

"O that is very reasonable, indeed," answered Owen. "I'll not buy any now, but will take a little of the odor."

Hay is cut by the hundred thousand tons from the spontaneous growth of grass, clover, and wild oats, on the hills and valleys.

The sales of butter, cheese, and poultry in Sonoma County alone, during the season of 1856, are estimated at five hundred thousand dollars.

The soil of California, as proved by successful experiment, is well adapted to the production of cotton, tobacco, sugar-cane, sugar-beet, and mulberry; and it is believed that rice will grow as well on her marsh lands as in China.

California is also destined to become one of the greatest fruit-growing countries in the world, and great attention is being given to the cultivation of the best varieties.

"There are now growing in the orchards of the state three hundred and twenty thousand five hundred apple-trees; six hundred and nineteen thousand nine hundred and ninety-three peach-trees; fifty-nine thousand one hundred and seventy-one pear-trees; twenty-five thousand two hundred and sixty-four cherry-trees; two hundred and seventy-one thousand eight hundred and fifty-five of varieties not specified; and one million five hundred and thirty-one thousand two hundred and twenty-four grape-vines."

There are but few countries so well adapted to stock raising of every kind as California. The valleys, and hills, and mountains are covered with grass and wild oats, and where stock can have free access to the range they will thrive the whole year without

NEW WORLD MARKET, CORNER OF COMMERCIAL AND LEIDSDORFF STREETS

being fed. The only period in the year when they are likely to suffer at all, is about one month, beginning with the first fall rains. The grass matures and dries on the ground, and remains good hay during the dry season, but is spoiled by the first rains; then, until the new grass is up, which is but a few weeks, the pasturage is not good.

The census returns of 1856 make the following exhibit of live stock in California:

"One hundred and six thousand nine hundred and ninety-one horses; thirty thousand six hundred and forty-one mules and asses; six hundred and eighty-four thousand two hundred and forty-eight cattle; two hundred and fifty-three thousand three hundred and twelve sheep; four thousand five hundred and forty-four goats; one hundred and eighty-six thousand five hundred and eighty-five swine; two hundred and sixty-six thousand three hundred and thirty-six poultry."

Wild game and fowl abound in California; elk, deer, grizzly bears, etc., wild geese, brants, duck, etc., by the hundred million.

Fisheries are becoming a fruitful product of the California coast. "A company of Portuguese in Monterey have gone into the whale fishery along the coast, and have taken from whales which they have captured since March, 1856, say eight months, sixteen thousand gallons of oil, which were sold for twelve thousand dollars."

"Salmon fisheries are carried on upon the Sacramento River for a distance of fifty miles, extending south from a point ten miles north of Sacramento City. The season embraces five months, from February to April, and from October to November, inclusive, of each year. There are about four hundred men engaged in this business, employing a capital of seventy-five thousand dollars. The number of salmon taken during the season of 1856 was estimated at four hundred and fifty thousand, nearly four thousand per day. The average weight is about fifteen pounds each, amounting in the aggregate to six million seven hundred and fifty thousand pounds, which, at twelve and a half cents per pound, the average price of the sales throughout the year, amounts to eighty-four thousand three hundred and seventy-five dollars. There are several establishments at Sacramento engaged in the salting, smoking, and packing of these fish for home consumption, and to supply the demand from abroad."

The bays and rivers abound in sturgeon and other fish in almost endless variety.

The lumber business is carried on extensively. Timber is not well distributed through the agricultural regions of the state; there are millions of acres, not only in the valleys, but on hills and mountains, without a tree or sapling; one vast meadow with a heavy growth of grass and wild oats just ready for the plow, without even the obstruction of a stone; but the farmer is dependent for fencing and fuel on other regions not quite so good for agriculture, so that the "independent farmer" has to make terms with the independent woodsman of the mountains. There is an inexhaustible supply of timber in the Sierra Nevada and coast range mountains, and much of it the heaviest timber ever seen since the flood.

"The product of lumber in several counties forms an important part of their resources. In Tuolumne County alone the sales are estimated to exceed eight hundred thousand dollars per annum. The number of mills in the state is three hundred and seventy-three, of which one hundred and seventy are propelled by steam, and two hundred and two by water. Cost of erection estimated at two and a half millions of dollars. Aggregate capacity is about five hundred millions of feet per year."

"In addition to the above, there are several mills in San Francisco and Sacramento employed in the sawing and dressing of lumber. The exports of lumber for 1854, 1855, 1856, amounted in the aggregate to one hundred and ninety thousand and twenty-six dollars."

"The number of grist-mills in the state is one hundred and thirty-one. The aggregate run of stone two hundred and seventy. Sixty-seven mills are propelled by steam, and fifty-four by water. The aggregate capacity per day of the water-mills is three thousand five hundred and fifty-two barrels; of the steam, five thousand two hundred and forty. Estimating the water-mills to be in operation six months of the year, and the aggregate capacity of the mills of the state is two million one hundred and seventy-four thousand nine hundred and sixty barrels per annum. The capacity of the mills of Sacramento, San Francisco, San Joaquin, and Santa Clara, is one million two hundred thousand barrels of flour per annum; twice the quantity necessary to supply the entire population of the state. The cost of the erection of the above mills is estimated at two million four hundred thousand dollars." There are various other manufactories in the state.

The San Francisco Sugar Refinery, employing one hundred and fifty hands.

San Francisco Cordage and Oakum Manufactory, in successful operation. The buildings connected with the works are of the most extensive and permanent character.

Pioneer Paper-Mill, thirty miles from San Francisco, in Marin County, with a capacity to turn off fourteen and a half tons per week. The cost of the establishment, complete, is about ninety-two thousand dollars."

"There are fourteen iron founderies at present in operation in the state, several of which are of an extensive character, and well supplied with all the appliances necessary for the manufacture of machinery of the heaviest description."

There are eighteen Tanneries at present in the state, employing capital to the amount of ninety-four thousand dollars.

The amount of capital employed by the different ferries of the state is estimated at three hundred thousand dollars. This amount does not include the cost of the steamers employed on the Sacramento and San Joaquin Rivers. There are one hundred and seventeen bridges constructed, the aggregate cost of which is about five hundred and fifty thousand dollars."

Ship-building is becoming quite an important branch of business in San Francisco.

There are distilleries enough in the state to produce a stream of liquid fire sufficient in volume and venom to kill all the people in it, the producers included. The limits of this work will not allow me to give a more definite and detailed account of the various manufactories above referred to, nor an enumeration of many others worthy of notice.

The mineral products of California, so far as reported by the state geologist, Dr. Trask, are, in addition to that of gold, of which the world in general has been notified, as follows: Silver, copper, iron, sulphate of iron, magnetic iron, platinum, chromium, (the fine chrome yellow, so highly prized, is manufactured from this mineral,) gypsum, nickel, (a metal extensively used in the manufacture of German silver, for wares and household utensils,) antimony, cinnabar, or quicksilver. New-Almaden mine, in Santa Clara County, is believed to be the richest in the world, yielding at this time about twelve thousand pounds per week.

Bitumen is found in large quantities in the southern part of the state. "There cannot be less than four thousand tons of asphaltum lying upon the surface of the ground in the Counties of Los Angeles and Santa Barbara alone, within a few miles of the coast. Its value, delivered in San Francisco, would not be less than sixteen dollars per ton, equal in value to sixty-four thousand dollars." Nothing has been done in this line of business as yet, for the reason, I suppose, that induced Robert Sears, a friend of mine, to give up the lime-making business. Robert spent a year in the manufacture of lime in Santa Cruz, and sent a large shipment, the result of his year's toil, of as good lime as ever was produced, to San Francisco. He came up in company with me, from one of my Santa Cruz trips, to San Francisco, full of hope, to draw his money, but, alas for poor Bob! the money-market was overstocked, and all the lime he had would pay but about half his freight bill. He immediately left for the mines, believing

SUTTER'S MILL.

that if he could produce gold instead of lime, he would be sure of his money.

Coal is found in abundance, and exhaustless stores of marble, granite, and burr-stones. These are all regarded as sources of mineral wealth to the state, most of which are yet undeveloped, quicksilver and gold being the only two which have attracted much attention. Gold is the staple of the country. Its discovery was made by James W. Marshall, in Coloma Valley, about sixty miles east of Sacramento City, in the month of January, 1848. This gold discovery was not subsequent to the treaty by which California was ceded to the United States, as has been asserted in my hearing, by men in high position, the said treaty not taking effect till the 30th of May, 1848; but the treaty was made before the news of the gold reached the treaty-making parties. Marshall was employed by Captain Sutter, to build a saw-mill. In the prosecution of his work he turned a stream of water from the river into the tail-race, for the purpose of widening and deepening it by the strength of the current. After the water was shut off Marshall saw, at the foot of the race, some shining yellow stuff, which had been washed out and exposed to view by the action of the water, and gathering a handful of it, he ran away and told his employer. The echoes of his voice shook the world, and all nations responded to his thrilling story, and sent their sons to assist him in digging his tail-race.

"The amount of treasure manifested at the port of San Francisco from 1849 to the close of 1856, is three hundred and twenty-two millions, three hundred and ninety-three thousand, eight hundred and fifty-six dollars;" but besides that amount, millions have been carried away in private hands. I remember, a few years ago, a party of returning Californians, in being conveyed in a boat from the landing to the steamer in Virgin Bay, were capsized, and many of them sunk like lead, with the weight of the gold belted about their persons; while their poor brothers, who, perhaps, had no gold to carry, were picked up and saved. A lucky miner once fell into the San Juan River, and finding that his bag of gold was too heavy for his body, he took it off, and clenched it in his teeth, but it immediately put his head under water, so he let go the hard earnings of years, and by the greatest exertions saved his life; according to the devil's scripture, "Skin for skin, yea, all that a man hath will he give for his life." Job ii, 4.

From the best available sources of information, it is estimated that the California gold mines have yielded, within the period above specified, "nearly *six hundred millions of dollars*."

There are various modes of mining, some of the

most prominent of which I will mention. Early miners in California confined their operations almost exclusively to *surface diggings* along the banks of the water-courses, or sufficiently near to be hauled to the streams for washing. At present *deep diggings*, by means of "shafts" and "tunnels," into the hearts of the hills and mountains, are carried on very extensively. This mode requires capital, but is much more permanent and productive than surface digging. These drifts or adits are seldom less than three hundred feet in length, and generally range from ten to twelve hundred feet, and many of them large enough to use a horse within for carrying the "pay dirt" to the sluices without.

Dr. Trask, state geologist, gives the following specimens of cost and profits of some successful operations of this kind:

"The cost of opening the Mameluke hill, near Georgetown, by the parties interested, exceeded forty thousand dollars, while the receipts for the same, during the period of little more than one year, has exceeded five hundred thousand. Another case is that of Jones's Hill, the opening of which has already cost above thirty-four thousand dollars, the receipts being above two hundred and eighty-four thousand dollars; and still another in the County of Nevada, (Laird's Hill,) the expense of opening which was nearly forty thousand dollars, while the receipts from it in June last had reached the sum of one hundred and fifty thousand; the resources of either are as yet in anything but an exhausted condition.

"The above is mentioned only for the purpose of conveying a better idea of the expenses and profits of what is denominated deep mining in this state; and the localities named form but a small proportion of the aggregate of similar workings. In the counties of Nevada, Sierra, Placer, El Dorado, Amador, and Calaveras, there are scores of adits and other workings of similar dimensions, which have already cost sums varying in amount from ten thousand dollars upward to the figures given above, and from which proportional profits have been derived."

River diggings are carried on but about six months in the year, while the rivers are low. The mode is to divert the stream from its channel, so as to work the river bed. This is done by "wing dams," so constructed as to carry the stream all to one side, and open to mining purposes a *part* of the original channel; but more extensively by building a dam across the entire river, and by throwing the whole stream into a large "flume," constructed of timber and plank, in size and strength sufficient to carry the entire volume of the river. I saw one a little below Downieville, which carried the whole of

Yuba River for nearly half a mile. Along those flumes there are a great many water-wheels, as large as the under-shot wheels of grist-mills, used for propelling various kinds of pumps for raising and carrying off the leakage and standing water in the original bed of the stream, and for raising water by means of buckets attached to the wheels, which is conveyed in small flumes to other mining localities in the neighborhood, and also for pumping the water out of claims in the low grounds along the rivers.

An immense flume, with its wheels, and pumps, and small flumes, together with the hundreds of men engaged in disemboweling the bosom of the ancient river, and dragging to light the hid treasures it had concealed, it may be, ever since the days of Noah, presents a very lively scene. All these works are generally swept away by the high tides of the "former rains."

The great desire of the miners to work out their claims, generally keeps all hands busy in getting out the gold till the floods come, and then there is but little opportunity left for saving any fluming timber or accompanying appliances. A member of a fluming company on the north fork of Feather River, told me that in the summer's work they did not make enough to pay expenses till the last fortnight of the season, when, from beneath a single boulder, they took out thirty thousand dollars. He showed me the hole whence it was dug.

As an illustration of the extent of such operations, we note the following:

"A portion of Feather River, in the vicinity of Oraville, is at the present time under contract for a distance of two hundred thousand feet, at an expense of four hundred and ninety thousand dollars."

Some idea of the extent to which *quartz mining* is carried on may be gained by an exhibit of the number and cost of the quartz mills employed. "The number of quartz mills in operation in the state is one hundred and thirty-eight, of which eighty-six are propelled by water, forty-eight by steam, and four by horse-power. The aggregate number of stamps connected with these mills is fifteen hundred and twenty-one. The cost of machinery is estimated at one million seven hundred and sixty-three thousand dollars."

The quartz rock is quarried out, broken up, stamped, and ground to powder, from which, by means of water and quicksilver, the gold dust is extracted.

Hydraulic mining is also carried on very extensively. The mode is to convey through a canvas duck hose, a volume of about twenty inches of water, with a fall of from thirty to three hundred feet, which presses the water through an iron or brass inch and a quarter nozzle, with a force that would knock a man down. This nozzle, in the hands of a miner who understands his business, directs the stream against the side of a mountain or hill, by which, in many localities, he can in one day wash down a thousand cart-loads of dirt. He first directs the stream near the "bed-rock," at the base of the hill he wishes to wash down, and, by thus undermining it, causes a "land-slide." When the foundations are thus swept away, and the side of a hill, with its huge boulders and mighty trees, breaks and tumbles with a crash and thunder like the roar of artillery, all hands have to stand from under. I witnessed such a crash one day near Coon Hollow, in El Dorado County, and when I saw and heard the hill coming toward me, I, with all the rest, beat a hurried retreat; when distant about fifty yards, and increasing the distance as fast as I could, a stone, propelled by the force of the falling hill, struck me on the heel, and for days I halted like wrestling Jacob. The same water thus used to wash down the dirt, carries it through the "sluices," and washes out the gold.

The sluices, which are from twelve to eighteen inches deep, and as wide as deep, are made of plank, and extend in length from one to three hundred yards; in the bottom of them are cross bars, called "rifle boxes," to catch the gold, while all the gross material is carried away by the stream. Along these sluices men are employed with forks and shovels, breaking the clods, throwing out the large stones, and otherwise assisting the water to disengage the gold from the mass of accompanying matter. Every day or two the good time for "cleaning the sluices" comes, when every variety of gold dust, and "scales," and "grains," and "big lumps" are gathered. This mode of mining pays largely in mining land so poor that a man, with "pick and shovel," could not from it earn his salt. Many locations which have been worked over by other modes of mining, are profitably re-worked by this mode.

Gold-mining of every description requires water, and hence the *dry diggings* could only be worked during the wet season, and the spring-time of dissolving snow, until, by artificial means, the water was conveyed from the rivers over high mountains, and across deep canons, to those dry districts. The vast extent of rich mining country of this kind has given rise to a distinct department of business in mining operations, which furnishes employment for a great many water companies, and profitable investment for a vast amount of money.

The extent of this department of business may be illustrated by the following statistical exhibit in regard to canals and ditches: "There are four thousand four hundred and five miles of artificial water courses for mining purposes in California, constructed at a cost of eleven million eight hundred and ninety thousand eight hundred dollars. In addition to these there are about nine hundred miles now in the course of construction. There are thousands of square miles of rich mineral land in the state, now lying almost valueless for the greater part of the year, which could, with the aid of enterprise and capital judiciously expended, be made valuable for mining purposes, and thereby secure an abundant return."

It is proper to add, that "the progress already made in the construction of these works has been, with but few exceptions, accomplished by the miners themselves." If the limits of this book would admit of it, I would insert a great many more facts and incidents in regard to mining operations. The information contained in this chapter in regard to the resources of California, is compiled principally from the official reports of Dr. Trask, state geologist, and the returns of the state census for the year 1856. I have a number of those reports and census returns in my possession, but I am indebted for the compiling of most of the statistics of this chapter, and some remarks in quotation, to "The State Register and Year Book of Facts, for the year 1857," a 12mo volume, published annually by Henry G. Langley and Samuel A. Matthews, of San Francisco, and James Queen, of Sacramento City. The Register is the most complete collection of California statistics of every kind ever published, and I would heartily commend it to every man who desires to study California. I shall now pass from the mines to illustrate life among the miners.

CHAPTER X.

LIFE AMONG THE MINERS.

California miners are a hardy, muscular, powerful class of men, possessing literally an extraordinary development of hope, faith, and patience, and a corresponding power of endurance. They have in my opinion done more hard work in California, within the last eight years, than has ever been done in any country by the same number of men, in the same length of time, and I think I may safely say double that length of time, since the world was made.

All that is necessary to convince any man of the truth of this position, is for him to travel through the mines and see what has been done, in the leveling of hills and mountains, filling up of valleys, the digging of about five thousand miles of ditches and canals through mountains on mountains piled, the construction of aqueducts across deep canons, or gorges, from mountain to mountain, and the hundreds of acres of "bed-rock" under the mountains they have laid bare, and scraped and swept like a ship's deck. He will be struck, too, with the wonderful facility and force with which a miner moves his muscles.

There is as much difference between the muscular action of a California miner and that of a man hired by the month to work on a farm, as between the agonizing, aimless movements of the sloth and the pounce of the panther. As an illustration of miners' hope, faith, patience, and endurance, I will instance the "Live Yankee Company" of Forest City. I was informed when there that, as an experiment, they commenced a drift into the mountain between that city and Smith's flat. The mountain was so high that it was impossible to prospect it by sinking a "shaft" to the "bed rock," the nearest way to the heart of the mountain being in a line from the base.

They soon encountered a strata of solid rock, as hard nearly as pig metal. The company having no capital outside of their muscular power and indomitable energy, had to get their provisions on credit, and worked in that drift, boring, blasting, and digging for three years before they got the "color;" but "struck a lead" at last, and were amply repaid for all their toil. They took out a single "lump," while I was there, worth seven hundred dollars.

The miners are not all successful, but they nearly all abound in hope and energy. I seldom ever met with one who had not a "good prospect." No matter what his past disappointments and losses had been, he was going to do first rate as soon as he could get his claim open, or his "pay dirt washed out." Even the little boys of the country partake of this spirit. A "lucky miner," determining to take his family back to the Atlantic side, came on as far as San Francisco, and while stopping at Hillman's Hotel, awaiting the day of embarcation, went out one night and fell among thieves, who robbed and murdered him. His body, three days afterward, was found in the bay. His poor widow was almost heart-broken, and her little miner boy, only four years old, when he heard that his pa' was dead, went to her and said, "Ma, don't cry! *don't cry!* we'll dit along. You won't have to beg, ma. Dist wait till I dit a little bigger, and I'll do up and dig a hole right down in the mountain, and det out the dold for you. Ma, don't cry; you won't have to beg."

That all miners are not alike successful, is a fact growing out of a variety of causes. Some chance to get richer claims than others. Some have better health than others. Working in the rivers is very injurious to health. Those rivers are fed by the leakage of mountains capped with perpetual snow, and are in midsummer almost as cold as ice-water. To wade and work in this ice-water from day to-day, under the burning heat of summer sunshine, freezing the lower extremities and scorching the brain, will severely try any constitution; but for the purity of the atmosphere, and general healthfulness of the climate, very few could stand such exposure at all.

A Baltimorean made five thousand dollars in the mines, and started to go home to his family, but was induced to go into a fluming operation, and spend a summer in the river. He concluded that it was no use to go home with but five thousand dollars, when by staying a few months longer he could double that amount. The operation was unsuccessful, and the poor man not only lost every dollar of his money, but by working in the water so much lost his health, and never got further homeward than to San Francisco. I found him there in the charity hospital just as he was sinking to the grave.

Many injure their health working in drifts, especially when they are working under leaky ground. I saw a tunnel, near Forest City, from the arch of which water came down continually, like rain torrents, and one of the men engaged in it had been down with inflammatory rheumatism, unable to move a limb for weeks. A sick man not only loses his time, but his purse, subject to the drainage of California rates of expenditure, very soon discharges all its dust.

Again, in some mining districts the cost of living is enormous. There are large towns, and thousands of miners, away in isolated regions so completely mountain-locked that the only way of access to them is by mule trails winding round dangerous rock cliffs, and over mountain heights which, to the uninitiated, would seem to defy the daring of the chamois. Everything that is used in those regions—clothing, provisions, mining tools, and machinery—is packed on mule back.

Packing has hence become a very extensive and profitable business. A pack train usually numbers from thirty to one hundred mules, each carrying a burden of about three hundred pounds, of every imaginable shape—bales, barrels, boxes, crates, bags, and everything that the necessities or luxuries of a mining city could demand. To live in such regions, therefore, costs perhaps fifty per cent. more than in places easy of accesss.

Again, many miners are very reckless; they sport, and spree, and waste their hard earnings. Others, again, spend all they make in "prospecting." The prospectors constitute a very large and useful class of miners. They are always dreaming of immense treasures of undiscovered wealth. No matter how well they are doing, when they get a few hundred dollars ahead they must be off, with pick, and pan, and miner's pack, and seldom ever stop till their money is gone, and then they set to work in one place again till they can make "another raise." They are constantly discovering "new diggings," and opening immense treasures for others to gather and enjoy, while they continue to toil and go, and toil and go again, enduring the greatest hardship, and labor, and poverty; living on hope, but dying in despair. They are very much like their hardy pioneer brothers who led the van of Western emigration, lived in log-cabins, supplied their families with plenty of wild game and "pounded cake," slept on their arms, and defended the outposts of civilization against savages and wild beasts; an honest, generous, noble set of men, who deserve much, but get nothing more than a plain subsistence, and generally die in poverty.

As a specimen of California prospecting, I will mention the case of my friend C. He arrived in San Francisco in 1850, and got employment at Mission Dolores in the brick-making business, which was his trade, at seven dollars per day, with the promise of steady work by the year. After making a few hundred dollars he became dissatisfied. Said he:

"I've not seen my mother for several years, and I can't stay more than a year or two in California; and I see plainly enough that in that time seven dollars per day won't make such a pile as I want."

So he gave up his situation and went to the mines, where *he knew* he could do better with even ordinary success, and, besides, stand a chance to make some "big strikes."

I met with him a couple of years afterward, and said: "Well, friend C., how do you get along?"

"O, pretty well," replied he; "I opened a first-rate claim in Mariposa County last year, but just as I got it in good working condition the water failed, so I had to let it lie over. When the time came that I could have worked it, I happened to be away up near Downieville, and having a good claim there I didn't go back to Mariposa. I have taken out a great deal of gold, but in prospecting from place to place I have spent it all; but I have some good claims which will pay big by and by."

Three years after that I met Friend C. in American Valley. "Halloo, my old friend; how do you get along?"

"O, pretty well," replied he; "but I'm not ready to go home yet."

"I presume your dear old mother would be glad to see you by this time."

"Yes, indeed, and I would be glad to see her; but I can't go home till I make something."

"Well, how near are you ready?"

"I don't know. I have made money; but in traveling from place to place I have spent it all. I have been up to Oregon since I saw you, and had a chance to get a first-rate farm there, if I could have stayed; but I had some rich claims in Mariposa, and thought I ought to come down and look after them;

but when I got there, I found that some fellows had jumped my claims, and I couldn't get them off without a great deal of trouble, so I came away and left them. I afterward opened a good claim near Yreka; but my partner was a disagreeable, quarrelsome fellow, so I sold out for a mere song, and came away. I've got a good prospect near Elizabethtown, which I think will pay well when I get it opened."

Another, with whom I was acquainted, who had not seen his family for six years, said to me one day: "For five years I have set a time to go home about every six months; but every six months has found me either dead-broke, or doing so very well I could not leave." But few of this adventurous class, the prospecters, will submit to the mortification of returning to their friends without money, and but few of them are likely ever to have enough at any one time to pay their passage home; while nearly all of them, with their mining skill, might make a fortune if they would remain in one place, and save their earnings.

The *social condition* of a large proportion of the miners of California has been bad, but is now rapidly improving. Separated as they have been from all socializing home influences, and especially from virtuous female society, reduced to constant toil and the roughest modes of life, they beçame rustics, and many of them became very vulgar and profane. Many men of fine mind and good education have laid all their intellectual strength under contribution for the manufacture of witticisms and vulgar sayings, adapted to the demand of a vitiated social taste, and spent their evenings in detailing them for the entertainment of the fun-loving crowds.

The introduction of virtuous women and good families is working a hopeful social reform throughout the mining regions. I heard a letter-carrier's salutation to a company of miners, which was vulgar and scandalous in the extreme. From the miners he came to the house at which I was stopping, and addressed the lady of the house in a most polite, chaste, and gentlemanly manner.

The *moral condition* of the miners is by no means what it ought to be. But very few of them are particularly anxious to go to heaven. I preached to a large assembly of miners one Sunday afternoon in the streets of Placerville, a flourishing mining city of six thousand inhabitants. In front of my goods-box pulpit stood a stage-coach, which was crowded to its utmost capacity with as many of my auditors as were fortunate enough to secure so good a seat. I endeavored to show the multitude before me their unfitness for heaven in their unregenerated state, their utter want of sympathy with God, or adaptation to the immunities of heaven. To illustrate the truth of my position, I said: "If God should dispâtch a rail-car train to the city of Placerville this afternoon to convey passengers direct to heaven, the conductor might whistle till the setting of the sun and not get one passenger. Heaven has no attractions for you. It is a place to which you don't want to go. Why, if the flaming steeds of Elijah's chariot of fire were hitched on to that stage-coach, and the driver cracked his whip for the heavenly country, every fellow in it would jump out;" and in a moment the coach was cleared, every man in it leaped for the street in an apparent fright, from the apprehension that, perhaps, Elijah's horses might be hitched to the stage, and they taken off to glory, a place to which they did not wish to go.

Sabbath-breaking and profane swearing are prominent in the catalogue of miners' offenses against the Lord.

Sunday in the mines was remembered only as a day for trading, recreation, spreeing, business meetings, and preparation for the business of the ensuing week.

It was very common to see large cards hung up in boarding-houses and business places, like this: "All bills paid up here on Sunday." That was the day for miners to get their blacksmith work done, and lay in their supply of provisions for the week; the day for holding public meetings for the enactment of miners' laws, or other municipal business. Under a general statute, every mining district enacts its own laws, by the voice of the majority, regulating all the mining claims of the district, as to size, conditions of pre-emption, etc. Under those laws they can sue and be sued, and everybody has to conform to them. Mining companies and water companies also did a great deal of their collective business on that day; and promiscuous masses of all sorts assembled at the hotels and drinking saloons, to drink and spree without restraint. What was worse, the standard of moral law was thrown down, and its authority denied. When we remember that a large majority of those men were educated in a Christian country, and that many had even been professors of religion, it is easy to see how quickly even a Christian people will relapse into heathenism, if deprived of the wholesome restraints and elevating influences of the Gospel.

In a preaching tour I made through the mines, as late as 1855, I traveled nearly a week without the privilege of any Christian association, and I longed for the opportunity of shaking a Christian's hand, and of feeling the warming sympathy of a heart that loved Jesus. On entering a mining town I inquired in the hotel at which I put up, whether there were any professors of religion in that town.

"Yes," answered the landlord, "there is one. Mr. T., our blacksmith, is a good Christian man."

And different boarders added: "Yes, Mr. T. is a

good man if ever there was one. He has his family here, and everybody looks up to him."

So, at my earliest convenience, I hastened to see Brother T. He received me very cordially, and introduced me to his family, all of whom looked very neat and respectable, and I rejoiced in the privilege of meeting so exemplary a Christian family away in those wild woods.

As soon as I took my seat I inquired of Brother T. how he was prospering in religious life.

"Well," replied he, "I think I am getting along pretty well, considering all the circumstances; but not so well as I did in Illinois, where I enjoyed the public means of grace. My greatest drawbacks here are my having no religious meetings to go to, and my having to work on Sunday. I support my family by blacksmithing, and the miners must have most of their work done on Sunday; and, to tell you the truth, I have worked in my shop here every Sunday except two for five years. One Sunday I was sick, and couldn't work; and one Sunday I went to hear the only sermon ever preached on this creek, which was delivered by Brother Merchant."

"O," thought I, "shades of the fathers! if this is the 'best man in these mountains,' the Lord pity the worst."

I traveled nearly a week before I found another Christian. He was an old ship-master, a good old

Methodist from Boston. I invited him to go to Long Bar, on north fork of Feather River, to hear me preach the following Sunday.

At the appointed hour, Sunday morning, I had a large audience to preach to under the shade of an ancient pine. The sound of the Gospel had never echoed through those hills before. Looking over my audience I discovered my old captain, and felt glad to think that I had at least one praying heart, who could sympathize with my mission and my message of mercy. After meeting I asked the old captain to take a walk with me "up into the mountain to pray." I felt that I needed the warming influence of a little prayer-meeting, and I supposed he did too. Finding a suitable place, I sang a few verses and prayed; I then sang again, and thinking I had got the good brother pretty warm, and that he in turn would contribute to the fire of my own heart, I called on him to lead in prayer. But I couldn't get a grunt out of him. Thought I, "Poor old captain, he is dried up."

I announced an afternoon appointment for preaching in the same place, and thought from the size of the morning audience, and the apparently good effect of the preaching upon them, that I would have a much larger congregation, and a better time, at the second appointment. But, to my surprise and mortification, I did not have more than twenty hearers, and when I cast about to know the cause, I learned that, according to custom, nearly the whole population of the neighborhood had by that hour of the day become too drunk to attend preaching. Such a variety of antics as they displayed beat anything I had ever witnessed. Next morning I found most of them sober, and ready to work; and to show their appreciation of my ministerial services, they gave me a donation for my Bethel cause of nearly one hundred dollars. The cases here given are to illustrate the general character of the miners in those regions. I found in nearly every place I visited honorable exceptions—sober, serious men, who deeply deplored the prevailing wickedness of the miners; and everywhere I went there was a general expression of desire for the regular preaching of the Gospel, and the establishment of its institutions among them, and a liberal support for a preacher and his family was pledged. I found a few merchants, too, who would not sell goods on the Sabbath. A man of my acquaintance, who passed for a minister of the Gospel before he went to California, opened a provision store in the southern mines. He commenced business with the determination not to sell liquor, nor to break the Sabbath. He had a moderate degree of success on that principle, but nothing to compare with the success of his business competitors, who sold liquor and kept open on Sunday. His pecuniary sense became shocked a great deal more by what he considered his losses, than his moral sense was comforted by his spiritual conquests. So, having mining friends to call and see him on Sunday, he was induced to leave his back door ajar, so that any who desired might be accommodated with a pair of boots, or a week's provisions. That paid so well that he was induced next to leave his front door ajar. He then in a short time, in accordance with that vulgar, dangerous, but popular maxim, "May as well be hung for stealing an old sheep as a lamb," set his doors wide open, and added the liquors to his supply. He felt that it was all wrong, but pleaded necessity, and thought that as soon as he could make a certain amount of money, he would quit the business, go home, and do good with his money. For a season he had extraordinary success, employed thirty yoke of oxen, all his own, on the road from Stockton to his place of business, to supply his store with goods. He had besides several hundred head of valuable cattle.

Finally, there came a night in which he was surprised by the Indians, who stampeded his cattle, burned up his store, goods and all, and the ex-reverend gentleman fled for his life, and begged his way down to Stockton as poor as Lazarus. He regarded his reverses as a judgment for his apostasy, and repented his fall. When I made his acquaintance he was in the honorable business of milling, making flour to supply his neighbors with bread, and was bringing "forth fruits meet for repentance." I heard him in a public meeting give a tearful narration of the above facts. Brother H., a friend of mine, opened a provision store in the northern mines. The first Sunday after opening, a company of miners came to get a supply of provisions at the "new store," but to their surprise they found the doors closed, and going in the rear, they found the new merchant in his tent.

"Halloo! old man, we've come to buy some provisions from you. We are very glad you have opened a store in these diggings; it's what we have wanted here for a long time."

"Well, boys," Brother H. replied, "I have opened a store here, and intend to keep a good supply of everything you may need; but I want you to understand from the start, that I will never sell you any liquor, and will never sell you goods of any kind on Sunday."

"Well, old man, you may just as well pack up your duds and go home, for you can do nothing here on those terms.

"You have a right to your opinion, boys," replied Brother H., "but I intend to do right, whether I make anything or not. If I can't make a living without poisoning my neighbor by selling rum, and offending God by breaking his holy day, I'll starve, or beg my way home; but I intend to give it a fair trial before I abandon the effort."

"Old man," rejoined the miners, "we are hungry, we ate the last of our provisions yesterday evening, and have come to get something to cook for our breakfast. Let us have enough to satisfy our hunger to-day, and we will come to-morrow, and lay in a supply for the week."

"Boys, you can fast and pray to-day," replied the old man, "and you'll learn, next time, to make timely provision for the wants of the Sabbath."

With that the miners got mad and swore a while at the "old fool," and left; but everywhere they went they told about an "old fogy who had come up into the mountains to teach us all how to keep Sunday." They thus advertised him all through those mountains, and thinking men at once came to the conclusion that a man maintaining such a position must be an honest man. "We can depend on the word of such a man as that. Rely upon it he won't cheat us." The result was that the better class of miners poured in upon him for supplies at such a rate, that in a few months he "made his pile," and returned East to his family.

Wicked as were the mass of California miners, they have always displayed some good qualities. They have all encountered hardships and sufferings, and most of them have hearts to sympathize with the suffering. Though appeals to their charity are of almost daily occurrence, yet no man in real need, that I ever heard of, has ever yet made a fruitless call on the miners for help. They are magnanimous, too, in their liberality; but they have an utter abhorrence of little, mean things; for example: There was a fellow at Smith's Flat, who, to gratify some secret brutal passion of his own, tied a chicken, and put it alive on the fire, and cooked it for his dinner. The thing was made known in the town, and the miners immediately called a meeting, and unanimously passed a resolution to the effect that the chicken-roaster's presence was no longer desirable in that camp, and that fifteen minutes be given him, after due notice from a committee appointed to notify him, for his disappearance from those diggings, never more to return. Several months had elapsed at the time of my visit there, but up to that hour he had not been seen in those parts after the expiration of the ominous fifteen minutes.

A butcher in the town of Alameda received a similar notice from a similar court, giving him two hours. About the middle of his last hour I saw him driving away with his effects in a wagon. Among his movables were several live sheep, one of which got loose in the midst of the town, jumped out, and ran for life. The butcher and one of his men pursued it a few squares, and finally shot it, threw it into the wagon, and was out of sight by the time his hour had expired.

Notorious rogues were often discharged from a town or mining camp in that way, while notorious murderers were hanged by the neck. Judge Lynch has transacted a great deal of business in California. I designed inserting a chapter of facts and incidents illustrating the history of Lynch law and Vigilance Committee operations in California, and the natural and Providential laws under which those facts have been manifested, but my space in the present book will not admit of it. However much may be said in condemnation of Judge Lynch's court and its proceedings, there is this to be said in favor of the denizens of California, that riots, and a promiscuous shooting into the masses, killing the innocent with the guilty, such as have been enacted in Baltimore and other Eastern cities, have never been known in California. Such, for example, as I saw last May in Washington City, when, to quell an election riot that had occurred and passed over without any mortal effects three hours before, one hundred and ten hired soldiers, with muskets each loaded with ball and three buckshot, fired upon an unsuspecting crowd of citizens, instantly killing eight unoffending men, besides wounding many others. That I witnessed, if, to be sure, getting up from my dinner-table just across the street and standing behind a brick wall to avoid being shot myself, may be called witnessing it.

Such riots, and such promiscuous shooting and killing I have never yet heard of in California. In the administration of California Lynch law, so far as I have known or heard, the thunderbolt of public fury has always fallen only on the head of the guilty man who by the enormity and palpable character of his crime excited it, and then not until after his guilt was proved to the satisfaction of the masses composing the court.

For example: A stranger called late one evening at the cabin of a miner who had his wife with him, and begged for lodgings, saying that he was a poor traveler, had been unfortunate in business, etc. The miner and his good wife pitied the poor stranger, took him in, and treated him to the best they had. The next morning after breakfast the miner had occasion to go away a few miles, and left the man at his house. When he got out of sight, the accommodated stranger murdered the woman and proceeded to rob the house. Before he got quite through, however, with his nefarious work, the miner returned, saw what was done, and raised the alarm.

The murderer was caught and tried. A meeting of miners was called to order, a judge appointed to try the case; witnesses were examined, and the guilt of the criminal proved, upon which the judge stated

UNIV.
OF
MICH.

HANGING OF JENKINS ON THE PLAZA.

the case and submitted the question of life or death to the mass composing his court, who unanimously voted guilty, and death by hanging. The judge decided that the criminal should be allowed fifteen minutes in which to prepare for death. He was then hung by the neck to a tree.

I give this fact without comment, simply to illustrate the character of Judge Lynch's proceedings. The accompanying cut will illustrate a similar tragedy, and the first of that kind enacted in San Francisco by the Vigilance Committee of 1851. Jenkins was hung from a cross-beam at the south end of "the Old Adobe on the Plaza," within a few feet of my pulpit. This is the "Old Adobe" to which frequent allusion is made in my "Seven Years' Street Preaching in San Francisco," from the front veranda of which, as seen in the cut, I for several years preached to the excited varieties of the world.

It is a fact, which I believe is generally admitted, that just in proportion as the LAW acquires power in California for the protection of her citizens, in that proportion Lynch law is dispensed with; and I believe that when the legal authority of the state attains to a degree of honorable dignity and strength sufficient for the accomplishment of its glorious ends throughout that commonwealth, Judge Lynch will resign his office, and forever decline re-election.

I would remark further in regard to the miners,

and the same remarks will apply to Californians generally, that they are a self-reliant, independent class of men, who, in all matters of personal opinion and conduct, think, and speak, and do as they are inclined, and cheerfully extend the same privilege to each other and everybody else. Hence ministers of the Gospel, in California's worst days, were permitted to preach in bar-rooms, gambling-saloons, public thoroughfares, or wherever they wished, without hinderance or disturbance.

For example: I went into the city of Sonora at nine o'clock one Saturday night, not knowing a man in the place; and finding the streets crowded with miners, who had gathered in from all parts of the surrounding mountains, I felt a desire to tell them about Jesus, and preach the Gospel to them; so I got a brother whom I chanced to meet, to roll a goods' box into the street, nearly in front of a large crowded gambling-house, and taking my stand, I threw out on the gentle zephyrs of that mild April night one of Zion's sweetest songs, which echoed among the hills, and settled down on the astonished multitudes like the charm of Orpheus. My congregation packed the street from side to side. Good order and profound attention prevailed, while the truth, in the most uncompromising terms, was being proclaimed. At the close of the exercises many, strangers to me, who had heard me preach in the streets of San Francisco, gave me a hearty greeting, among them a notorious gambler, who shook my hand and welcomed me to the mountains.

I preached in Jamestown one night under similar circumstances. I got permission of a butcher to convert his meat-block into a pulpit; I tried to have the butcher himself converted, but did not succeed in that, though he made very humble confessions, and, like Herod under the preaching of John, "did many things." Selecting the best point for a crowd, I happened again to be in front of a large gambling-house. Some of the gamblers, thinking that I was putting on too strong an "opposition line," took offense and tried to run me off the track. They knew the character of the miners too well to attempt to confront the preacher personally; so to try and scatter my audience, they tied some tin pans to a dog's tail, and sent him off with a clatter, they yelling after him. Stopping short in the midst of my sermon, I said:

"There they go, poor fellows; they want to make their souls happy. Rather a poor intellectual entertainment, tying tin pans to a dog's tail; but I presume it's the best they can do, so we'll let them go and make the most of it."

By that time they were out of sight, out of hearing, and the attention of my audience stimulated and improved.

The social and moral condition of the California

miners has been gradually improving for the last four years. Mining operations have already assumed a degree of local permanency, which to many would be considered impossible. When a man opens a drift into a good lead he has before him, in working out his claim, profitable employment for a dozen years.

The deep diggings, hydraulic and quartz mining, are all carried on for years in the same locations; and in many places the miner can calculate in advance the returns of a year's labor, as certainly and definitely as can the mechanic, merchant, or farmer. The mining towns commenced eight years ago, and which it was believed would be abandoned to the coyotes in two or three years, as the mines in those localities would be worked out, have generally gone on, increasing in size and permanence every year, and bear now as hopeful indications of living to the end of the world, as do the agricultural and commercial towns. I am not speaking of the paper towns and cities peddled about in numberless scores by speculators, but which never had an existence except on their beautifully colored maps; the mining towns I have in my mind when instituting the above comparison, are such as Nevada, Grass Valley, Columbia, Sonora, each containing an average of five thousand inhabitants; and a hundred others of various sizes, equally prosperous and permanent.

The miners everywhere through the mountains are settling their families; schools and churches are multiplying in every direction. Besides the ministers of other denominations, who are doing a great work for God, there are upward of ninety itinerant preachers in connection with the California Conference of the Methodist Episcopal Church, who are sounding the jubilee trump from Dan to Beersheba, from Yreka to San Diego. Gambling has gone down, under the pressure of an indignant public sentiment, a thousand per cent. below par, and all the "hells" in the state were closed three years ago by the hand of the law. The great Goliah of Gath, the gambling fraternity of California, which defied all Israel for years, has fallen, and his decapitated carcass has been delivered over to the vultures. The Sabbath is honored much more now than formerly, and though many, very many and great evils remain, yet social and moral progress are now the order of the day in California.

CHAPTER XI.

CALIFORNIA AS A MISSIONARY FIELD.

God, in his word and in his providences, has revealed and established two leading modes of spreading the tidings of salvation to perishing sinners of distant lands. The first is to send the Gospel to them in heathen lands, by his embassadors; and the second is to send them to the Gospel in Christian lands, by his providences.

The Divine authority of the first mode is found in the great commission: "Go ye into all the world, and preach the Gospel to every creature;" but the apostles receiving it were to tarry at Jerusalem, until endued with power from on high. By the time the power descended upon them, God, in his providence, developed the second mode. When the apostles came down from that celebrated upper room, from that extraordinary protracted prayer-meeting, with hearts of love and tongues of fire, lo! right at their doors were assembled representative dwellers of at least fifteen different nations. These all listened to Peter's great pentecostal sermon, and not only heard and saw the "wonderful works of God," but felt in their hearts, that very day, the power of pardoning grace, and away they went back to their homes, declaring everywhere the great things which had come to pass in the "Holy City," and "holding forth," in the experience and conduct of a new life, the torch of redeeming love in the darkest and most remote portions of the earth long before the preachers had even noted one foreign mission on the plan of their appointments. God was beforehand with them then, as he has been ever since.

The fact is, their views in regard to foreign missionary work and the redemption of the race were, as yet, so contracted, that they would not preach the Gospel to any but Jews, even at home, until by the exhibition of the "great sheet," with its animals of every kind, St. Peter's sectarian shackles were unloosed, and he was compelled, by the direct command of God, to go and preach to the house of Cornelius. St. Paul was the first foreign missionary to go abroad and establish missions among the heathen, and make a practical demonstration of the first mode referred to; but in nearly every place he visited, he found scattered abroad the pentecostal seeds of truth, which had been borne, as it were, on the wings of the wind by the efficient workings of the second mode.

Without stopping to show that those two modes of missionary enterprise bear respectively the sanctions of Divine providence in every age of the Church's history, I would simply say, that never, perhaps, since the days of St. Paul, have they been more clearly exhibited than at the present hour. The planting and sustaining of Christian missions among the heathen and semi-heathen nations of Europe, Asia, Africa, and Oceanica, are in strict accordance with the first mode. Foreign missionary work, therefore, is Scriptural in its authority, and therefore necessary, and must be sustained at whatever cost, however long we may have to wait to see the fruits of an abundant harvest. The practical results, however, arising from the labors of foreign missionaries, of all Christian denominations, are, upon the whole, hopeful and cheering. They survey and plot the unoccupied territories of Immanuel's lands, establish militant posts, and garrisons for soldiers of the cross, and bear the truce-flag of redemption to the uttermost parts of the earth. Foreign missions are worth more than the cost of sustaining them, for the influence they exert on the commercial adventurers and seamen of Christian nations. Many a prodigal son has been arrested and brought to Christ in foreign lands by Christian missionaries, who could not, perhaps, have been reached anywhere else. I will give one single case to illustrate this position. A. M. Brown, a sailor of my acquaintance, was extremely wicked and profane, an avowed enemy of

Christ and his Church, and especially of missionaries in foreign fields. He openly opposed the missionaries at the Sandwich Islands, Navigator's Islands, and other islands of the Pacific, and did everything in his power to throw obstructions in their way. From the Pacific he shipped to Constantinople, and was there, a few days after leaving the vessel, seized with the cholera, and under the dreadful shock fell helpless and alone in the streets. I have heard him say: "While I lay there in the streets of Constantinople, dying, as I believed, I thought on my past life, and awoke to a sense of my dreadful condition as a sinner; I felt that I should soon be in hell; despair, with all its horrors, seized my soul; and thinking that it was then too late to pray, I said to myself, Why didn't I attend to that before? Why didn't some one kindly warn me of my danger? I had a father, who once made a profession of religion, but he never told me what a dreadful thing it is to die in sin, and go to hell. Why didn't some preacher, or some Christian friend tell me of all this? No man hath cared for my soul, and now I'm dying in the streets of a foreign city, and going to hell. And," said he, "in an agony of despair, I cursed the day of my birth, and cursed my father for his neglect, and cursed the preachers, and cursed the Church; and then my paroxysms of pain would come on, and I writhed under the scorching rays of the sun till life was almost gone; and when I had a little respite, I thought of my mother, and wept, and said, 'O, if I had a mother's care, or if I had anybody who could understand my language, I could tell them what to do for me, and I might yet live. The Turks would stop and look at me, and jabber to each other and pass on.

"When all hope had gone from me, a man, whom I supposed to be an Englishman or an American, came and looked at me, and I thought, O that he would speak to me in a language I can understand! He spoke to me; but, alas! it was in the Turkish language. Seeing that I could not understand him, he addressed me in my own mother tongue; such music never thrilled my soul before. He spoke, too, such words of kindness and sympathy as never before fell on my guilty ears. He had me taken up and conveyed to his house, and under his skillful treatment and care I was relieved in a few hours. That good Samaritan was an American missionary. He saved my life; and, more than that, he led me to Christ. Three days after my recovery, while still at his house under his instruction, God, for Christ's sake, spoke my sins forgiven, and healed my soul."

From that day Brown became a steadfast, zealous Christian. He was for several years a local preacher in my charge in San Francisco, and one of the most efficient workmen I had.

I received a request from the "Hawaiian Tract

Society," a few years ago, to send them a colporteur for Honolulu, Sandwich Islands. I sent them A. M. Brown, who fulfilled his engagement greatly to the satisfaction of the society, and successfully preached the Gospel in the very port where once he had so wickedly opposed it.

But however important and glorious the foreign missionary work, I believe that the greatest achievements of American missionary enterprise are now in progress, and will ere long be accomplished, through the second mode, above indicated. "The abundance of the sea" is now being "converted," and used, more effectively than ever, for the great purposes of the Gospel. The nations are flowing together as they never did before, and flowing especially in all their variety to Protestant America.

The tide of emigration from European nations has been rolling in for more than a century, and now the tide from Eastern heathen nations is bearing its tens of thousands to our Pacific shores. What glorious Gospel achievements have already been gained among those resident on our shores, and how wonderful the reflex power of them on kindred and friends in the various lands whence they came, and how many, like the "Parthians, and Medes, and Elamites, and dwellers in Mesopotamia," etc., have gone back to tell of the "wonderful works of God," through all the countries whence they came. Mark the success of American Christian missions in the Republic of Liberia. See the success of Methodist missions among the Scandinavians in this country, and the missions now being successfully established by converted Swedes and Danes, in Denmark and Sweden. Especially note the extraordinary success of Methodist missions among the Germans, first in this country, and then, by a kind of reflex power, in the "Father-land," waking up the German mind from the dreams of rationalism and dead formality. The German missionaries sent back from this country to Germany, have accomplished more good within the last twelve years, by preaching the Gospel in their vernacular language, than the same number of men of any other nation or language could have accomplished there in fifty years. They now have a mission conference there, which held its first session in September, 1857, Bishop Simpson presiding.

The Methodist mission in China was commenced about the same time that Brother Jacoby was sent back to Germany, and after all the toil, and expense, and sacrifice of life which have been given to the Chinese mission, those zealous missionaries have never yet been able to report the conversion of more than six Chinamen. I do not mean to institute any invidious comparisons, or to say one word against the Chinese mission.

The mission is necessary and must be sustained,

CHINESE FEMALES.

but what I wish to say is, that if the Lord in his wise providence has no other mode for the conversion of China, it will be a long time before her three hundred and sixty millions of heathens will hear the Gospel. Let any man fond of arithmetical calculations tell us how many men, and how much money, and how long a period of time will be required for the conversion of the Chinese Empire by the present mode?

But let the wisdom and mercy of God be adored, he has another mode which is already beginning to shed the light of hope on the future of China. The Missionary Society is supporting a few men in China, who have to devote half a dozen years in acquiring the language so as to gain access to the Chinese mind, and then a dozen years more will be necessary to wear off their prejudices against foreigners, so as to give them access to the Chinese heart.

But, in the mean time, God in his providence has forty thousand long-cued fellows in California, at no expense to anybody, studying the English language, through which the Gospel message will reach their hearts, and then, they, by the thousand, it may be, can return on the principle we have illustrated, and carry the tidings of salvation to the perishing millions of their own land. True, but little has been done as yet, in the way of direct Christian effort, for the conversion of the Chinese in California. Rev. William

Speer, of the Presbyterian Church, formerly a missionary in China, built a good brick Chinese Church in San Francisco, organized a small society of Chinamen, preached to them for several years in their own language, organized a Sunday school among them, where they were taught the rudiments of the English language, and also, for a time, published a Chinese paper in San Francisco. Mr. Speer's health failing, he has for a season suspended his labors. Rev. Mr. Shuck, of the Baptist Church, formerly a missionary in China, has built a Chinese chapel in Sacramento City, where he, in connection with a pastoral charge of his own people, preaches to the Chinamen in their own language. Besides those two enterprises, I know of no direct organized effort for the salvation of the men of China. A Methodist preacher takes hold of one sometimes and teaches him letters, and gives him Gospel teaching. Rev. S. B. Rooney reported a very hopeful conversion of a Chinaman at our conference in 1856.

But though so little direct effort has been put forth by the Church in this direction, still, much has been done, and the way is being prepared, in the order of Providence, for their conversion by and by. They acquire our language with considerable facility. They soon become impressed with our superiority over them, and so soon begin to give up their national prejudices and exclusiveness. When a Chinaman

CHINESE MERCHANTS.

arrives in San Francisco, with his turban cap, wide trowsers, and wooden shoes, he enters with the prevailing idea of his people, namely, that he belongs to the most enlightened, enterprising, and pious nation under the sun; but after he stares a few days at our magnificent buildings, gas-lighted streets, and machinery of various kinds, our splendid steamers, etc., and sees the enterprise and energy exhibited by Americans, and others whom he always before regarded as barbarians, he wilts right down like Jonah's gourd, feels as though he was nobody, and all his people in the same class with himself. The next idea which seems to strike him, is that perhaps he may, having such models to work by, become somebody after all, "be same as von Melican man;" and the next time you see him you discover that he has shed off his native costume as clean as a snake in spring-time, and has come out in full American rig—hat, coat, pants, and the biggest boots in town. The self-conceited, prejudiced, haughty Chinaman has been converted into "von Melican man," with a full desire and purpose to learn, and talk, and be "just same as any other Melican man."

From that time he begins to learn the English language and pry into everything.

I preached one night in the summer of 1855 in M'Ginnis's provision store-room, at Twelve Mile Bar, on the east branch of the North fork of Feather

River. A large proportion of my congregation were Chinamen, who appeared to listen with great attention. Among them there was a tall intelligent-looking fellow whom they called "Chippee." I was told that he had been in the country only about six months. Chippee not only appeared to listen attentively, but took out his pencil and went to noting down such thoughts as he could gather from the discourse, on a piece of wrapping-paper which lay on the counter, as gravely as a New-York reporter. The next morning the clerk of the store observed him transferring his notes from the wrapping-paper into a book or journal, and asked him to translate them into English.

Then said Chippee: "What you call him talk las night?"

"That was Mr. Taylor, from San Francisco," replied the clerk.

He noted the name in his book, and then said, looking and pointing upward: "What you call him, *Him*—Fader, big Fader, up! up! What you call HIM?"

"We call him God," answered the clerk.

So he noted that in his journal also.

He then gave the following brief translation of his notes from the wrapping-paper, which I now have in my possession:

"Tell all men, no gamble; tell all men, no steal

em gold; tell all men, no steal em cargo; tell all men, no talk em lies; tell all men to be very good men."

That was the first sermon Chippee ever heard, and those were the ideas he gathered from it. What the spirit of inquiry thus awakened in his mind may lead to, who can tell? But besides the forty thousand Chinamen referred to, whose numbers are every year increasing, we have in California the representatives of all other nations. What St. Peter saw in *vision*, on the house-top of Simon the tanner, is exhibited in *fact*, in California, and none of them common or unclean, nor excluded from the covenant of mercy, but all are subjects of redeeming love, and living objects of the Saviour's sympathy and intercessions.

What I said of the Chinese is true of the rest; they are learning our language and our civilization, and the way is opening for their reception of the Gospel, and thence they may bear the news to the ends of the earth. It has been my lot to preach the Gospel hundreds of times, if not to every creature, at least to specimen representatives of all the creatures, I suppose, of human kind in this lower world.

The following account of preaching the Gospel to all the world in San Francisco is given in the "Annals;" due allowance must be made for the writer's poetical allusion to the singing on the occasion:

"Suddenly from the piazza of an old adobe on the Plaza arises the voice of one crying in the wilderness. He 'raises' a hymn in a voice which would be dreadful in its power were it not melodious. Hark! you may hear the words half a mile off. The City Hall sends back the echo like a sounding-board. You may stand at the foot of Merchant-street and distinguish every sentence: 'The chariot! the chariot! its wheels roll in fire!' Had the vehicle spoken of really rolled over the planked streets of the city, it is doubtful if the tumult of its lumbering wheels could have drowned the voice of him who was thus describing, in thunder-like music, its advent.

"That voice at once arrests attention. The loiterer turns aside from his careless walk, stops, and listens. The miner, in his slouched hat and high boots, hears the sounds of worship, recollects the day, thinks of the home and the dear ones far away, and of the hours when he, too, worshiped with them in the old church pew, in the country town, with the graves of the rude forefathers of the village visible from the spot where he sat; the old elm-trees bending gracefully beneath the weight of years and foliage, over the dust of those who planted them; and where he listened to the trembling words of the gray-haired old clergyman as he read, or spoke from that old-fashioned pulpit, and he joins the motley crowd.

The loafing Mexican arouses from his reverie, and from the smoke of his cigarette, gives an extra puff from his nostrils, throws his variegated *serape* over his left shoulder, leans against the fence, and listens to words which he does not understand.

"John Chinaman passes along, and, seeing books, and being of a literary turn, ceases to jabber in the language of Confucius, joins the outskirts of the company, and risks the integrity of his yard-long *queue* among the 'outside barbarians.'

"The Malay, with his red-pointed cap, stops a moment to wonder, and, perhaps, forgets a while the well-known trade of piracy when listening to a Gospel which he cannot comprehend.

"It is not long ere there is a sufficient audience. The singing has brought together the congregation. There is room enough for all. The worship progresses. Prayer, singing, reading of the Scriptures, text and sermon follow. All can hear, all can see; there is no sexton nor usher, nor is one needed. It is a primitive service, very earnest, and by no means ridiculous."—P. 671.

I think I never felt a greater thrill of pleasure in proclaiming a free Gospel to the human varieties of California, than I did one Sunday morning a few years ago on Long Wharf in San Francisco. It happened that morning, when the time came for my wharf appointment, that I was minus a text. I was caught in the same embarrassing dilemma once before, on my way to preach on the Plaza, but as I passed along I saw a poor inebriate lying in the sand, with his face downward, drawing with every breath the sand into his nostrils, and as temperance sermons were in order occasionally on the Plaza, being a place notorious for rum holes, I resolved, as I looked at the poor fellow, to preach that afternoon a sermon on temperance. When I had sung up my crowd, I said to them: "You may find the text recorded on a sand-bank in front of the General Jackson House, in First-street."

Then said I, "It is usual in sermonizing to institute inquiries something like these:

"I. What are the facts in this case?

"II. What are the causes or occasions of those facts?

"III. What are the consequences?"

With that arrangement I proceeded and had a good time, but waked up a great excitement among the rum-sellers. Opening our fires right at the mouth of their dens, there was no popping at a man of straw, or sham-fighting. When I succeeded in making out a case, I pointed out my man, and the home-thrust of the prophet Nathan to the guilty king of Israel, "Thou art the man," was backed by the concentrated gaze of a thousand listeners. Such thrusts were hard to bear, but harder to resist, and the guilty, after one cry of complaint, usually got out of sight.

On the Sunday morning above referred to, I found no drunken man to suggest a theme, but I met a brother who said, "Good morning, Brother Taylor; what's the news this morning?"

"Good news, my brother, good news! Jesus Christ died for sinners." Said I to myself, "I've got it."

So on I went, and took my stand on the head of a whisky barrel in front of the worst rum hole in the city; if there could be a worse one it was at the opposite corner, just across the street. I guess the latter was the worst, for they would not let me preach in front of it. I preached there a few times, and the proprietor sent me word that I blocked up the street, and cut off access to his house, and he didn't want me to preach there any more.

The next Sunday after I received his message, I stood on a pile of wood about thirty feet from his door, and by way of apology for changing my pulpit, said to the people: "That man there complains that I block up the entrance to his house, and forbids my preaching there any more. He is a gate-keeper of the way to hell, and is bound to keep the passage clear, so that all who are silly enough to go to hell may walk in without hinderance. He's a generous soul, is he not? Moreover, a man who steals God's holy day, and spends it in the work of human destruction, can't afford to lose an hour of it."

Then the proprietor of the opposition death line on

the other side of the street, sent me word that I might preach in front of his place. He rued his bargain once or twice, and tried to run me off, but I stood fire, held my ground, and turned his empty whisky barrels to good account, by preaching perhaps a hundred sermons from them.

On the occasion I was going to describe, I sung together a vast crowd, of such a variety of human kind as never was seen except in California. Peter's congregation on the day of Pentecost, for *variety*, was but a small affair compared with it. When the songs ended, I said: "Good morning, gentlemen; I am glad to see you this bright Sabbath of the Lord. What's the news? Thank the Lord, I have good news for you this morning: 'Behold, I bring you good tidings of great joy, which shall be to all people.'" I then addressed them as individual representatives of the different nations thus: "My French brother, look here!" He looked, with earnest eye and ear, while I told him what Jesus had done for him and his people. "Brother Spaniard, I have tidings for you, señor," and told him the news, and requested him to tell his people. "My Hawaiian brother, don't you want to hear the news this morning? I have glad tidings of great joy for you, sir." I then told him the news, and that his island should "wait for the law" of Jesus, together with other "isles." "John Chinaman, you, John, there by that post, look here, my good fellow, I've got something to tell you," etc. Thus I traveled, as it were, over all creation, calling by name all the different nations I could think of, recognizing their representatives before me, and I felt unspeakably happy in the fact, that throughout creation's vast realm I could not find a rebel to whom I could not extend the hand of hearty Christian sympathy, and say, I have good news to tell you, my brother, "glad tidings of great joy, which shall be to all people." When I had got round, as I thought, an Irishman in the congregation spoke out and said:

"And may it plase your riverence, and have ye nothing good for a poor Irishman?"

"Why," my dear Irish brother, "I ask your pardon, sir," I replied, "I did not mean to pass you by. Thank the Lord, I have good news for you, my brother. Jesus Christ, by the grace of God, tasted death for every Irishman on the Emerald Isle; and let me tell you, my brother, that if you will this morning renounce all your sins, and submit to the will of God, Jesus, your Saviour, will grant you a free pardon, and clean all the sins and all the devils out of your heart as effectually as your people say St. Patrick cleared the snakes and toads out of Ireland."

"Thank you, sir," said he, "I raly belave ivery word you say, and I'll try and be a betther man."

There is, beyond a doubt, a spirit of inquiry at

work in the dark minds of heathen and semi-heathen foreigners in California, in regard to our institutions, civilization, and religion; and when they become familiar with our language, and with our Bible, the light will break upon them as upon the mind of Martin Luther, when he found the chained Bible.

An intelligent-looking Italian came to me to know where he could get an Italian Bible. "A Spanish Bible will do," said he; "I can read Spanish pretty well, but I prefer an Italian Bible, as I want to read to my companions." He informed me that he was one of a party of twelve Italian refugees, who took part in the revolution of 1848, and had to flee for their lives; said that he and his party had been in California eighteen months, and had often heard me preach in the streets, and were anxious to become acquainted with our Bible and the Protestant religion. They liked the preaching so far as they could understand it, and thought that was just the religion the Italians needed. I went with him, and he got a Bible from a branch depository of that glorious institution, the American Bible Society.

The Italian afterward told me that he and his companions were delighted with the great things they found in the Bible. He said they spent their evenings in reading and talking about it.

Those fellows despised oppression. I saw a Spaniard in Clay-street one day beating his little boy.

Several of those Italians happened at the time to be on the opposite side of the street, and as soon as they heard the cries of the little fellow, they ran across the street, and knocked the Spaniard to the pavement almost as suddenly as if he had been shot, and took charge of the boy. I happening to know the boy, took him by the hand and conveyed him to his mother.

The next time I saw the Italians, they ran across the street to meet me, and inquired very particularly about the welfare of the little boy for whom they had fought.

A company of Maltese lived near me for several years. I gave them a Testament, and told them about St. Paul's shipwreck and sojourn on their native island, and how well their ancient ancestors treated the servant of God. They seemed as much delighted with the book as if I had given them the family records of their fathers.

A company of Manilla men wintered near me during the winter of 1849–50. I used to tell them about Jesus, and they attended my preaching in "the highways." They could not, at that early day, understand much English, but to show their appreciation of their preacher, when in the spring they were about leaving for the mountains, they brought me a present, consisting of a variety of their native tools, etc.

One Sunday, as I was preaching in Washington-street, I observed in the congregation an old Italian weeping. At the close of service he grasped my hand:

"O, dat what I like; tell everybody 'bout Jesus; I never saw such free preaching and free Jesus before. O, I likes it! When you preach again?"

"This afternoon, on the Plaza, at four o'clock," said I.

"O, I'll be there! I likes it!"

"Are you acquainted with Jesus?" said I.

"O yes, bless de Lord, I'se got him right in here," replied he, putting his hand on his breast; "I loves him wid all my heart."

I saw him at preaching several times afterward. He always took his stand close in front of me, and gazed, and listened, and wept, and seemed to enter almost into the spirit of good old Simeon. I have no doubt that he enjoyed the pardoning mercy of God, and was ready, like Simeon, at the call of his Master to say: "Lord, now lettest thou thy servant depart in peace, according to thy word: for mine eyes have seen thy salvation, which thou hast prepared before the face of all people; a light to lighten the Gentiles, and the glory of thy people Israel."

At an experience meeting in our Seamen's Bethel in San Francisco, a Prussian arose, and said:

"I come to California to git golt; now I don't care about de golt; I want to find dat Yaesus you all talk about. I believe he is my friend too, and I want to find him. De handt of God has been heavy upon me since I be in California; he shakes me, he shakes me now. I dream de odder night dat I was dying, and a great pig snake had me, and just as my breadt was almost gone, Brodder Taylor came along and knock de snake away, and help me up. I didn't know Brodder Taylor den, but dis is de man dat knock de snake off, and dis is Brodder Taylor. De snake is de debil; O Brodder Taylor, and all you brodders, will you pray for me, and help me get away from de debil, and find Yaesus?"

We all prayed earnestly for him, and he was clearly converted to God. As soon as he found Jesus, he said he wanted to go back to his own country to tell his mother about Jesus; and about a year afterward he took passage, saying he was going home to tell his mother about Jesus. I have seen a number of Scandinavians converted in San Francisco; and the first thing a converted young Dane, or Swede, or Norwegian talks about when he finds Jesus, is his "dear mudder." They want to go straightway and tell "mudder" all about it.

We have, in connection with Yreka station in Siskiyou County, about four hundred miles north of San Francisco, a class of, I believe, eighteen Methodist Kanakas, Sandwich Islanders. They have one of their own men for leader; and Brother Stratton, who was their pastor a couple of years, represented them in conference as being very pious and consistent, attended class regularly, and contributed voluntarily and liberally for the support of their pastor. And while the masses of Americans around them paid no regard to the Sabbath, those converted heathens spent it only in songs of praise, and in other religious exercises. There are many hinderances to oppose the spread of the Gospel among the heathen and semi-heathen of California, especially the example of God-hating, Christ-rejecting, Sabbath-breaking, over-reaching, profane English and Americans, the leading representatives of Protestant Christian nations, whose influence has spread over the land a universal moral blight, which for a time seemed to consume, like the locusts of Egypt, every green thing.

But now, thank the Lord! the spring-time of religious life has come; much that seemed to be dead has revived, and all over the country are seen buds and blossoms, and "fruit unto holiness;" and songs in the vales are heard, like the songs of the ancient captive people of God when returning and coming to Zion. Notwithstanding all past and present obstructions, the Church may command greater facilities for the conversion of the heathen in California than she can have in a foreign field. In the first place, as we have shown, their contact with American ingenuity and energy knocks their national pride and prejudice into the dust, and they are almost imperceptibly, as by a ground swell, borne up on the tide of American civilization. They at once feel that they are dependents, and soon become imitators of their superiors. Thus some of the greatest obstructions to the foreign missionary's success are carried away before the Church makes a direct effort for their salvation. Again, a foreign missionary cannot, ordinarily, till after many years of labor, exhibit to the heathen the light of Christian example, except that of his own experience and conduct. He has no means of giving them an example of the practical effect of religion in society. There are many persons, even in Christian lands, who think that religion is only suited for preachers and men of leisure, and not at all adapted to the active relations of business and social life, and such a conclusion would be most natural to the mind of a heathen. To place a foreign missionary, therefore, on anything like equal footing, in this regard, with the Church in California, we must export to his field of labor Christian merchants and mechanics, blacksmiths, carpenters, etc., and Christian farmers and housewives, etc.; in short, a Christian colony.

In California the heathen are learning, and will yet learn more perfectly to discriminate between the mere subjects of Christian nations, and the Christians in fact; and there the missionary has at once the advantage of a living exemplification of Christianity in every department of business and social life, to set before his heathen brother.

Let any man weigh the facts we have in part indicated, and he will see that the gold magnet of California was pointed by an all-wise and merciful Providence, for the purpose of attracting and enriching the nations, not in gold, but godliness ; and that when these "strangers and foreigners" shall have acquired our language, and some knowledge of the institutions of Christianity, a Pentecostal gust of glory may burst upon them, and they by thousands see and experience "the wonderful works of God," and return to their homes God's own embassadors, to carry the truce flag of redeeming mercy to their perishing brethren, and declare to them in their own vernacular tongue, the royal proclamation of peace and pardon through the blood of Jesus. Upon a careful review of the foregoing facts, taken together with the proximity of California to the heathen millions of Asia, and Japan, and Oceanica, etc., and her constant inter-communication with them, I come to the deliberate conclusion that California is to-day, in the openings of Providence, the most important missionary field under the sun. "The harvest truly is plenteous, but the laborers are few: pray ye therefore the Lord of the harvest, that he will send forth laborers into his harvest."

CHAPTER XII.

BIT OF EXPERIENCE — CONCLUSION.

For the information of my friends who inquire why I am here, five thousand miles from my conference, and my California field of labor, and when I expect to return, I will very briefly insert a bit of my experience.

After organizing the Powell-street Church in San Francisco—the first Methodist Episcopal society in California—which I served two years, I was appointed to establish in that port a seamen's Bethel enterprise, which was to comprise the erection of a large *church* for the seamen and sojourners of the nations who were constantly thronging our streets, and the establishment of a *home* for the shipwrecked and destitute mariners of all seas as they were crowded upon us. I commenced without a dollar's worth of patronage from any source, except what spontaneously sprang up in the streets of that city in connection with out-door preaching; but we proceeded in the name of the Lord and the people, and within a period of two years we completed a church forty by ninety feet, plain and substantial, the best church at that time in the state, besides a good parsonage, and had a church property worth in the market, above all indebtedness, thirty-four thousand dollars; and, what was better, the Lord was with us in great mercy, awakening and converting sinners, so that the "Bethel enterprise" was considered the most glorious work connected with our conference.

Up to this time the Home department of the enterprise had not been commenced, while the necessity demanding such an institution in that port was keenly felt from the beginning. Finally, in the progress of improvements in that part of the city, an opportunity presented itself by which the trustees of our enterprise saw clearly, as they believed, that if they could obtain a loan of the funds necessary to put up the Home building, that certain available resources in hand (the nature of which we have not room here to explain, nor is it necessary) would in due time refund the money, and we would then have our enterprise completed and out of debt, without having to make any further demands on public benevolence; a most desirable consummation.

The trustees found, however, that while moneyed men were satisfied with their securities—the lot on which the Bethel stood, and the one on which they contemplated the erection of the Home—they were not willing to take the names of a Church corporation. They demanded, in connection with those securities, a responsible personal name. "Father Taylor's" name was proposed and accepted. It was a matter of no secular interest to me, and involved a heavy pecuniary responsibility; but having long before consecrated myself to the Lord and his cause, and shrinking from no responsibility that seemed necessary and safe, and the basis being considered by all parties ample security against all contingences, I consented to that arrangement, got the funds without difficulty, and made the proposed improvements, my conference indorsing it as one of the grandest enterprises of the day. So it seemed to all observers in the light of California progress at that time.

For a season everything went on prosperously, but a tide of reverses soon set in, affecting the business of the entire state, depreciating everything, and especially San Francisco real estate. In the midst of the pressure along came a devouring fire, which swallowod up our late improvements in an hour, and our "broad and reliable basis" had by this time narrowed down by the general depreciation until, like the prophet's bedstead, it was quite too short to allow a long man, straitened out with such responsibilities as I had to bear, "to stretch himself on it, and the covering narrower than that he could wrap himself in it;" and now an unthought of alternative began to stare me in the face, more dreadful to my feelings than a dozen of deaths. Two days after the fire a noble band of San Francisco merchants met together "on 'Change," and having looked over the facts and figures of our sinking enterprise, came up to the question of relief with an enthusiasm and generosity which were characteristic of merchant princes. Said they: "This man must not be allowed to suffer. We know how he has preached here five times a Sabbath, and labored day and night for the improvement of society in this city for half a dozen years, and here are the official documents to show that he never could have been benefited one cent by this enterprise, had it been as successful as was contemplated; and now to allow him to sink under its unforeseen and uncontrollable reverses, is a thing to which we will never consent." That was the talk, I assure you. It came like the voice of hope to a drowning man. They accordingly appointed a committee of four of the best men in the city, in my opinion, to raise by subscription the funds necessary to rebuild and carry our enterprise through. That committee, after meeting together, and looking over the ground, reported to me that they would forthwith raise ten thousand dollars, and then stand by and see that I should not suffer. A mountain was rolled off my heart, and I returned home that day, feeling like a man just converted and saved from impending perdition. But my rejoicing was of short continuance; for only two days after that, before my committee could commence their work, Page, Bacon, and Co.'s bank, and immediately Adams and Co.'s bank, with their branches throughout the state, banks of world-wide celebrity and unquestioned solvency, went down with a crash, followed by a train of banking institutions and business firms, till the panic arose and swept through the state like a hurricane in a forest.

My friends, by the hundred, and most of my trustees, were thrown into tangled prostration, and buried in the common ruin. The few friends who were left were like the standing oaks in the forest after the fury of the tornado has passed, scathed, peeled, and slivered, holding their position firmly, but having no sap to spare for their dying neighbors. So I was now caught in what a Californian would call "a very bad snap," and how to get out was the question. My committee and a few others did nobly; but after a few desperate struggles we had to succumb. Everything was surrendered but the church, without a lot to stand on; and I went up to conference with a full exhibit of the facts and figures from the commencement, which were examined by that body of ministers and pronounced correct; but the unanticipated extraordinary reverses had swept the board, pay day had come, and there was nothing in the "locker." Those California preachers are, upon the whole, as noble a set of fellows, in my opinion, as the Lord ever made, and they would have footed the bill and helped me right up if it had been possible; but it should be remembered, that in the space of half a dozen years we had supplied, at an enormous expense, exceeding that of any other new country, about fifty circuits and stations with churches and parsonages; and though we had gone as strictly as seemed practicable, on the principle of "pay as ye go," we were, nevetheless, nearly everywhere more or less behind, and all suffering from the general panic, so that nearly every preacher came to conference with a church or parsonage on his back, or a crushing weight of reponsibility on behalf of "our paper" and university, and each wondering how upon earth he was going to get rid of his burden. We were like a set of shipwrecked mariners, each cast forth on a broken fragment of the wreck to drift or paddle ashore as best he could; and all we were able to say as we floated near each other was, "The Lord bless you, my brother! I hope you'll get ashore. I'm sorry I can't help you." They passed a list of resolutions of confidence and condolence on my behalf, very good in their place, but they would not pay any debts. The report of the "Committee on the Bethel," which was adopted by the conference, closes with the following preamble and resolution, a certified copy of which I have:

"*Whereas* the Rev. William Taylor, at the request of the trustees of the Seamen's Bethel, assumed heavy personal liabilities for the Bethel enterprise; and *Whereas* this conference, at its session in Sacramento City, 1854, did give their sanction to the Bethel enterprise and said arrangement; and *Whereas*, by fire and depreciation of property, the enterprise financially failed, and involved Brother Taylor to an amount above assets of twenty-two thousand fifteen dollars and thirty-five cents; therefore,

"*Resolved*, That we deeply sympathize with Brother Taylor in said involvement, and regret that it is not in our power, personally, to assist him.

(Signed) "Isaac Owen,
"John Daniel,
"M. C. Briggs,
"G. S. Phillips. } *Committee.*"

Now, what was a poor Methodist preacher to do in such a case as that? Must I be sacrificed on the altar of my devotion to the cause of God and humanity, and go down into the dark sea of bankruptcy without hope, or fall back on my own resources, and say, It shall be settled? I chose the latter alternative. And my resources, what were they? What little property I had was dried up in the general depreciation, so as not to avail one copper.

My resources consisted of a well-developed physical constitution, six feet high, and a heart full of the love of Jesus, and Gospel hope and faith. With these I said to the Conference: "Brethren, I am fully persuaded that God, in permitting this train of reverses to befall our Bethel enterprise, has higher and better ends in view than our pecuniary success, which he will bring to light in due time; but the honor of the cause demands that at some time this whole business be satisfactorily settled. However great the mistake in running any risk in the premises, the Lord knows the purity of the motives underlying the whole matter, and I believe he will in mercy permit such a settlement; and in view of all the facts, I have made up my mind to "face the music," trust in God, and settle it. How or when the Lord only knows, or how much he will enable me to pay, I cannot tell; but enough to satisfy all parties concerned under the circumstances, and vindicate the honor of his cause."

In the midst of those reverses I had, for the first time in my life, an attack of rheumatism, which kept me in doors a few days; and being unable to do anything else, I tried my hand in writing out a few death scenes; and finding that my pen went much easier than I expected, I became interested and encouraged, and in connection with my regular pastoral work, I found in a few weeks that I had matter enough written to make a book.

On the eve of the session of conference to which I have referred, it struck me one morning that I ought to go to New-York and publish my book, and it might become the entering wedge toward relieving my embarrassments; and moreover, that, with twelve years' experience in street-preaching, I might by my example, in connection with my book on that subject, enlist the sympathies of the Church more fully on behalf of the ten millions of outsiders in the United States, for whom there are no church accommodations. The more I thought of it, the more plausible it seemed; but there were two apparently insurmountable difficulties in my way. First, I could not leave without the consent of my conference, and I knew they had no men to spare; and second, I could not go without money to pay my passage. To leave my family would cost more than to take them with me, and that would cost, with myself, about seven hundred dollars; quite an item for a man who had not money enough to take him fifty miles to conference and back. But when I started to conference I submitted the matter to the Lord in this way: I said to the Lord, that if it were his will and my duty to go East, I would take two facts as an expression of his will, and never doubt. The first was the advance of the passage money, and secondly, the consent of my conference.

I was not presumptuous nor enthusiastic; I did not expect the Lord to work a miracle, or anything of that sort, for my accommodation; but I did not know of a friend I had "unbroke," to whom I could go for the money; and I knew that it was a law in the spiritual kingdom, not to send a man to wage "a warfare at his own charges." At any rate I was willing to leave the case in the hands of the Lord, and let the decision of the question, to go or not, turn on those two conditions.

Strange as it may appear, without solicitation, and most unexpectedly, I received on the second day of the session of conference, the following note from Judge Haven, a noble, high-minded outsider, who had known me and my labors from the commencement:

"San Francisco, *Aug.* 26, 1856.

"My dear Brother Taylor,—The Mail Company will take you and family, for $675, and knock off $375, leaving $300, which I have to-day collected for you, so that it will cost you nothing to get home.

"Yours truly, J. P. Haven."

I read it and said, "Thank the Lord for that; I think I see in that an important link in the chain of Providence." On the last day of the session

I informed the brethren that I had written a book; told them my convictions of duty in regard to going East, the unexpected supply of the passage money, etc.; so the conference voted me leave of absence, which was sanctioned by the presiding bishop. The conference then passed the following preamble and resolution:

"*Whereas* the Rev. William Taylor, an honored and useful member of this body, has prepared materials for a work, to publish which it appears necessary that he should visit the Atlantic states, for which purpose he has obtained leave of absence from this field for a time, therefore,

"*Resolved*, That the Rev. W. Taylor has our confidence and sympathy, our commendations and our prayers, and he shall find willing hands to clasp him and warm hearts to welcome him on his return.

Signed, "M. C. Briggs,
"E. Thomas,
"J. D. Blain."

We came to New-York as strangers in a strange city, in which the high rates of boarding very soon exhausted our little stock of funds; and when our little California boy died we had not money enough to bury him. It was Christmas day, and while the multitudes were rejoicing without, I sat with the partner of my missionary trials, triumphs, and reverses, in the house of mourning; and as we wept over our dead, she inquired, "William, how much money have you left?" "Two dollars and seventy-five cents; not enough to buy a coffin for our dear Willie." But we knew in whom we had believed, by whom we had never been forsaken in the darkest storms we had ever seen. We looked to our Father in heaven, and he sent us sympathizing friends in our need. A good brother bought us a coffin, and hired a hack, in which we conveyed our boy to the house of the dead, and thanked God for comfort in the dark days. Then, again, when I tried to get my book through the press, I could not find a publishing house that would touch it without the cash; a thousand dollars must be paid as soon as the work was done, and I had not a dollar in the world; but I made a contract on the faith that the Lord would help me some way; so the night before it was necessary to close the contract, up turned a live Californian, a merchant prince, who knew me and my cause, and said he, "Gó ahead, Taylor; I'll back you;" so out came the book. While getting that book through the press it struck me that I could write a better one, but I was so occupied for a year after, that I could get no time for writing, except one week in Philadelphia, last summer, having but six sermons to preach, I sat down and wrote, "ADDRESS TO YOUNG AMERICA, AND A WORD TO THE OLD FOLKS," a little book which is selling well, and, I believe, doing good. And when confined last fall with small-pox, isolated from society as utterly as if I had the leprosy, I wrote a chapter on Social life in California for my contemplated book, but when I got out I immediately went to work in the great revivals of the season. I assisted in conducting some heavy campaigns, and everywhere had glorious victories, and became so absorbed in the great business of soul-saving that I got quite out of the spirit, and about out of the notion of writing another book, and had engagements for several months ahead; but in the midst of a siege in Stamford, Connecticut, I was attacked with rheumatism, the second attack of my life, but much more severe than the first. I was knocked off the track completely, and finding myself incapable of field work, my attention was again called to my contemplated book; so when the extreme severity of the rheumatic shock had passed, I went to writing, and now, as the pains are leaving me, I am finishing my last chapter.

In regard to my return to California, I have only to say, that I expect to return from choice. I labor for the salvation of sinners as cheerfully and earnestly in one place as another, but my family are homesick to get back to California, and I prefer it to any other country, both for myself and for my boys, and I am held here only by the pressure of the mission for which I came. I travel from city to city, and have no home for my family. We have buried one boy, as I have before remarked, since our sojourn here; nursed another last spring through scarlet fever; nursed two others last fall through small-pox, self and wife down with varioloid at the same time; so we find this mode of itinerancy anything but agreeable. We are, nevertheless, greatly comforted by several considerations.

First, The Lord is with us in great mercy, and has cheered us with his comforting presence during every hour of our reverses and afflictions, and has graciously sanctified them all to our spiritual advancement.

Secondly, Though absent from my conference and my adopted field of labor, I am, nevertheless, at work in the vineyard of God, preaching regularly, in doors and out, except during the periods of confinement referred to, from eight to twelve sermons a week, and have had the happiness of seeing many hundreds of souls converted.

In the third place, I am doing more for the relief of my needy cause than I can hope to do in any circuit or station, and hence feel it my duty to work on in this way till my cause is relieved, or till my duty in some other direction is clearly indicated in the order of Providence. If I had a few "kinsmen" here, or in California, who could redeem their brother, and let me up from this crushing responsibility, I would be free at once to go into the *regular* work in California, or wherever else the Lord might send me. What is past in my experience, I know; what is to come, is with the Lord and the people. I believe I am, in the order of Providence, through a train of reverses, well ballasted, and am ready, most unhesitatingly, to respond to the Lord's call for any voyage: "Here am I, send me."

It was my design in this book to finish my story in regard to the "Book Concern of the Pacific;" to tell of the California Christian Advocate, its life, death, funeral expenses of nine thousand dollars, and its resurrection in time to publish to the world the first notice of its own death; in short, I designed giving specimen exhibitions of missionary life in California, from the commencement down to the present period. I also designed giving life-takings of individual men and women, personal adventures, perils by sea and land; well-authenticated thrilling facts and real scenes, illustrating California life in all its departments. Also some account of ancient relics of history, government works, charitable institutions, and to tell of the natural wonders of the land —its sublime mountains, crowned with crystal and eternal snow, whose tears water the vales in summer heat; its mineral springs; its streams and waterfalls; Yohamite Falls, the greatest wonder of the kind in the world, leaping from mountain heights four times the distance of Niagara; its giant trees, the largest, I have no doubt, the Lord ever built; and especially the seasons, perfect transparence and purity of the atmosphere, and the salubriousness and variety of California climate.

But my book is full. In missionary life I have but briefly illustrated the first seven months coming under my own observation. I have only "prospected" and "opened" a rich historic mine, running through a period of more than seven years, which yet remains to be "worked out," besides the lateral "drifts" to which I have just referred.

Now, in view of these facts, I feel inclined to add another volume. If I can command the time, and the public demand will justify the expense, a second volume of "California Life Illustrated" shall be forthcoming.

THE END.

SEVEN YEARS'
Street Preaching in San Francisco,

EMBRACING

INCIDENTS AND TRIUMPHANT DEATH SCENES.

TESTIMONY OF THE PRESS.

"AMONG the first of our noble army of occupation in California was the Rev. William Taylor. In labors he has been more abundant, and as fearless as laborious. His book, as a book of mere incident and adventure, possesses uncommon interest; but as a record of missionary toil and success its interest is immensely increased. The sketches of personal character and death-bed scenes are thrilling." —*Ladies' Repository.*

"The observation and experience recorded abounds with the most pleasing interest, and the scenes are described with much graphic power and felicity."—*Baltimore Sun.*

"This is a graphic description of the labors of a missionary among the most complex, and perhaps most wicked, and at the same time excited and active population in the world. It is a very rich book, and deserves a large sale."—*Zion's Herald.*

"As a religious history, it occupies a new department in Californian literature; and its incidents and triumphant death scenes are of the most interesting character."—*The American Spectator.*

"It is a very entertaining volume, full of adventure, grave and gay, in the streets of a new city, and among a peculiar people."—*New-York Observer.*

"This work is valuable, not merely from its very sincere and sound religious spirit, but from the curious popular traits which it imbodies, and the remarkable insight it affords into the striking and highly attractive peculiarities of the Methodist denomination. We defy any student of human nature, any man gifted with a keen appreciation of remarkable development of character, to read this book without a keen relish. He will find in it many singular developments of the action of religious belief allied to manners, customs, and habits all eminently worthy of study. The straightforward common sense of the author, allied to his faith, has resulted in a shrewd enthusiasm, whose workings are continually manifest, and which enforces our respect for his earnestness and piety, as well as affording rare materials for analysis and reflection. The *naïveté* of the author is often pleasant enough; in some instances we find it truly touching."—*Philadelphia Bulletin.*

"We like the spirit and daring of the author of this book. But few like him live among men. With an undoubted piety, and courage like a lion, he preached Christ at a time, in San Francisco, when Satan reigned about as triumphant as he ever has on any other spot of the cursed earth. The book will be read, and it will do good wherever it is read."—*Buffalo Chr. Advocate.*

"This book is a real contribution to the religious history of that country. For raciness of style it is one of the most readable books that has fallen into our hands."—*Pittsburgh Chr. Adv.*

"The state of society which Mr. Taylor describes is almost anomalous, and his pictures are boldly and clearly drawn"—*New-York Evening Post.*

Similar opinions to the foregoing have been given by the Western, Southern, and Richmond Christian Advocates, Christian Advocate and Journal, National Magazine, Methodist Quarterly Review, Harper's Magazine, and many others.

www.ingramcontent.com/pod-product-compliance
Lightning Source LLC
LaVergne TN
LVHW010201110826
845151LV00002B/579

* 9 7 8 1 4 2 5 5 3 5 5 5 1 *